# TALES OF OLD BATAVIA

## Treasures from the Big Durian

### Kami Ehrich

"It is my greatest desire to return here to see all these things, poke about these ruins, drop bits of soap down the volcanoes to see if they will go off as do the geysers in Iceland. This is in truth one of the richest and most interesting countries in the world, and so easily got to, so that I do hope I can one day return for a long stay."

*C.D. Mackellar*
Scented Isles and Coral Gardens
*1912*

EARNSHAW
BOOKS

## Tales of Old Batavia

### By Kami Ehrich

ISBN-13: 978-988-82734-9-2

Design by Coco Huang

This book has been reset in 10pt Book Antiqua. Spellings and punctuations are left as in the original edition.

HIS048000 HISTORY / Asia / Southeast Asia

EB065

Published by Earnshaw Books Ltd. (Hong Kong)

# Acknowledgments

Creating a book like this one involves searching through thousands of pages of books and pictures and attempting to quickly scribble a note along the way. We have tried to be as thorough as we can in recording sources and citations, but it is possible that some have been missed. Should you find any item lacking a citation or incorrectly attributed, please let us know so we can make the appropriate changes to future editions. We believe all items included are out of copyright or are used within the bounds of fair usage.

I received a great deal of help in creating this book, especially from Adil Hakim. I would also like to thank Graham Earnshaw and the people at Earnshaw Books for the opportunity to put this book together and their invaluable support along the way.

*Kami Ehrich*

# Introduction

The city of Jakarta is today the capital of Indonesia, but it has had other incarnations, most notably as the regional headquarters of the Dutch East Indies, when it was known around the world as Batavia. Hence the name of this book. As the capital of the Netherlands' highly unlikely empire in the far east of Asia, Batavia was for 200 years the lynchpin for the spice trade. Even earlier than that, the city went by many other names including, when it was under the rule of a Hindu potentate, Sunda Kelapa, and Jayakarta when it later came under Islamic rule. After independence, the city's name was changed to Djakarta, but in 1972, the "D" was removed and it has ever since been known as Jakarta.

When they arrived in 1619, the Dutch destroyed the existing city and rebuilt it under its new name, Batavia, which derives from a region of the Netherlands, far, far away on the shores of the North Sea. It was built specifically to be the center of trade and commerce in the region,

as controlled by the Dutch. It was the capital of the Dutch East India Company and later the Dutch East Indies, which made fabulous amounts of money for the Dutch primarily from the sale of spices harvested from the thousands of islands in the territory. At one point, more trade was running through Batavia than in all of the other ports in colonial Asia put together. It was a bustling hub of commerce with all of the diversity expected of a center of regional trade.

Batavia, as the capital of the Dutch East Indies empire, was the source of power and authority to all residents on the almost 20,000 islands that made up the territory. The experiences of the almost 300 ethnic groups across the islands mixed with those of the European, Arabic, and Chinese populations that were drawn to the city through trade to create a rich history.

Before the arrival of the Europeans to the islands of the East Indies, they were home to Hindu, Buddhist, and Islamic kingdoms that thrived in the tropical paradise of Java. In terms of the European latecomers, the Portuguese were the first to arrive, followed closely by the Dutch and then the British. The islands, prosperous and thriving, were the ultimate prize for the countries looking to colonize what they knew, somewhat patronizingly, as the Far East.

The islands (for instance, the only location in the world for nutmeg production) had the European powers battling for control. But it was the Dutch who were victorious and they built an empire through the islands through the Dutch East India Company, which has been called the world's very first multinational corporation. At its heart was Batavia.

The company and its primarily Dutch employees seemed to have little time or interest in the richness and beauty of the islands. It saw only opportunity for profit and in its pursuit of a monopoly, committed gross acts of violence, destroying the landscape and massacring populations. Yet there were also many visitors and long-term foreign residents who were dazzled at the beauty of the nature and the culture of the local peoples. The islands were mysterious and magical with the jungle climate and unique biodiversity, hidden Buddhist and Hindu ruins, and relaxed local way of life. And Batavia was the gateway to this wonderland.

You will notice that what follows in this book is not confined to just the city of Batavia. It includes items that relate to many other parts of what was the Dutch East Indies and is today Indonesia. Looking at the region as a whole makes sense given the crucial role that batavia played, and continues to play under its new name. The various cultures, languages, and religions on the islands have all come together to form one nation, adding a richness and diversity that is embodied in the city of Jakarta.

The following collection of stories, images, and anecdotes are taken largely from European travelers and residents of the city. Through their words I hope you will appreciate, as do I, the beauty of these islands and the extraordinary history of this great city.

*Kami Ehrich*
*January 2015, Shanghai*

*Advertisement to join the Netherlands East Indies army in 1912*

# Chronology

| | |
|---|---|
| 1200 | Sunda Kelapa, an inlet on the Ciliwung River on the east coast of Java, becomes the main port of the Hindu kingdom of Sunda |
| 1300-1500 | Islam enters the islands through Sumatra and spreads, overtaking Hinduism and Buddhism as the dominant religion |
| 1509 | The first Portuguese ships arrive, marking the start of Europe's trade with the East Indies |
| 1522 | The Sunda Kingdom and the Portuguese sign an agreement giving the Portuguese control of the spice trade |
| 1527 | The Sultanate of Demak, a Muslim kingdom on Java, conquers Sunda Kelapa and renames the city Jayakarta |

*Weltevreden Station, Batavia*

| 1596 | First Dutch expedition reaches the islands with intentions to trade and, despite Portuguese interference, brings back spices to Europe |
| --- | --- |
| 1602 | The English East India Company establishes a trading post at Bantam, on the western end of Java |
| 1602 | The Dutch East India Company is established |
| 1603 | The Dutch establish a trading post at Bantam |
| 1611 | The Dutch East India Company sets up a trading post at Jayakarta |
| 1619 | The Dutch East India Company attacks and destroys the city at Jayakarta and rebuilds it, renaming it Batavia |
| 1621 | The Dutch massacre local people on the Banda Islands to reinforce their control over the nutmeg trade |
| 1623 | The Dutch kill 10 British subjects at Amboyna, a culmination of tensions between the trade rivals |
| 1667 | The English and Dutch sign the Treaty of Breda, giving the Dutch the last British-controlled island in the East Indies and a monopoly on trade in nutmeg and other spices in exchange for the island of Manhattan |

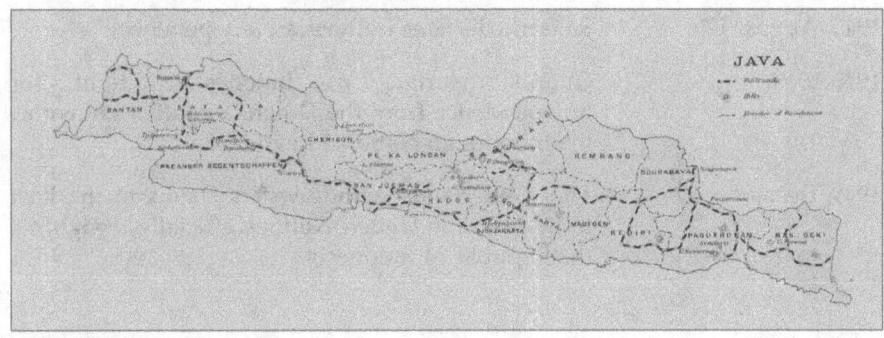

*Map of the Island of Java, 1907*

9

| | |
|---|---|
| 1699 | Coffee beans are brought by the Dutch from Yemen to Java and coffee plantations are founded on the island |
| 1712 | First shipment of Java coffee arrives in Amsterdam |
| 1740 | The Dutch massacre many of Batavia's ethnic Chinese population, a response to Chinese uprisings |
| 1800 | The Dutch East India Company goes bankrupt and formally dissolves, all holdings are nationalized and the colonial Dutch East Indies are established |
| 1811-1814 | The British briefly control the Dutch East Indies during the Napoleonic Wars |
| 1815 | Mount Tambora, on Sumbawa Island to the south of Java, erupts creating a global volcanic winter |
| 1883, August 26-27 | Mount Krakatoa, on Krakatau Island off Java's northern coast, erupts |
| 1930 | Future President Sukarno gives a series of nationalist speeches entitled "Indonesia Accuses" while on trial for his work with the pro-independence Indonesian Nationalist Party |
| 1941, December 8 | Netherlands declares war on Japan |
| 1942, February 27 | The Battle of Java Sea marks the beginning of Japan's occupation of the East Indies |
| 1945, August 17 | Sukarno declares Indonesian independence |
| 1945-1949 | Guerilla warfare as Indonesians fight for Independence from the Dutch, a conflict known as the Indonesian National Revolution |
| 1949, December 27 | The Netherlands withdraws its claims to the East Indies and the United Nations officially recognizes the Republic of Indonesia |

# What's In a Name?

The city once known as Batavia, and known today as Jakarta, has been called a few different names in its past. During the Kingdom of Sunda period, it was called Sunda Kelapa, meaning "Coconut of Sunda" in the language of the dominant race in this region of the island of Java, the Sunda people. During the short period of the Banten Sultanate around 1527, it was called Jayakarta, Djajakarta or Jacatra, the word from which the city's current name is derived, a word which comes from the Old Javanese and Sanskrit languages meaning "victorious deed", "complete act", or "complete victory". The Dutch took over the city in 1619 and under their colonial rule it was known as Batavia. Batavia was the name of a part of what is today the Netherlands during the Roman Empire, inhabited by the Germanic Batavi people. It was also the name of a Dutch ship that visited batavia at the beginning of the Dutch involvement. During the Japanese occupation from 1942 to 1945, it was called Djakarta or Jakarta and following Indonesia's independence in 1949, the city was formally renamed Djakarta before finally becoming Jakarta in 1972.

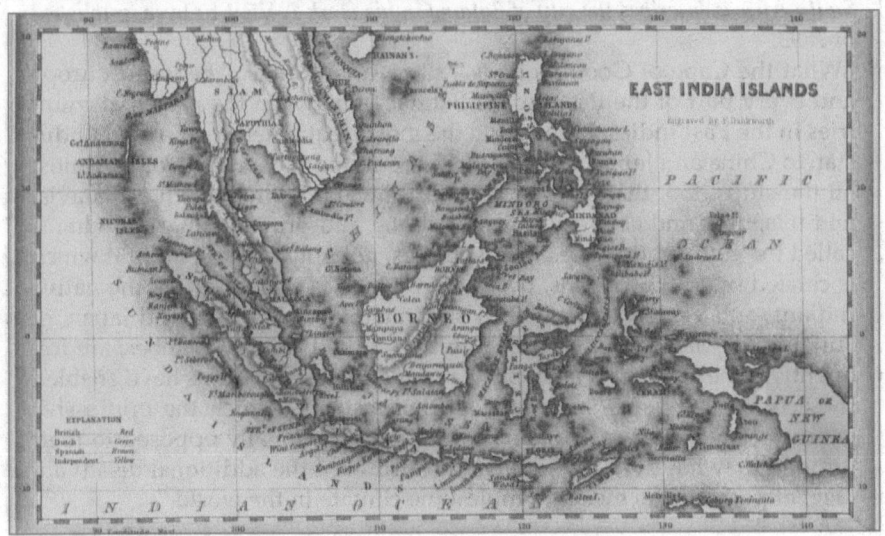

# The Center of Trade

*W. Basil Worsfold, an English scholar and writer best known for his work on South Africa, describes the city of Batavia in his work* A Visit to Java, *published in 1893*

"What the Cape of Good Hope is," says Adam Smith, "between Europe and every part of the East Indies, Batavia is between the principal countries in the East Indies. It lies upon the most frequented road from Hindustan to China and Japan, and is nearly about midway on that road. Almost all the ships, too, that sail between Europe and China, touch at Batavia; and it is, over and above all this, the centre and principal mart of what is called the country trade of the East Indies, not only of that part of it which is carried on by Europeans, but of that which is carried on by the native Indians, and vessels navigated by the inhabitants of China and Japan, of Tonquin, of Malacca, of Cochin China, and the Island of Celebes, are frequently to be seen in its port. Such advantageous situations have enabled these two colonies to surmount all the obstacles which the oppressive genius of an exclusive company may have occasionally opposed to their growth: they have enabled Batavia to surmount the additional disadvantage, of perhaps the most unwholesome climate in the world."

# Nightlife in Batavia

*Thomas H. Reid, a traveler to Batavia in September 1907, writes about the hotels and nightlife of the city in Across the Equator,* A Holiday Trip in Java, *published the year following his trip.*

Batavia is favoured in that it has a choice of several good hotels. Whoever selects the Hotel Nederland or the Hotel des Indes will say that the other "best Hotels in the Far East" have something yet to learn in the accommodation of visitors, general cleanliness, and moderation of prices. After sundown, so far as Europeans are concerned, with the exception of the little life seen under the electric light of Raffles Hotel and the Hotel de l'Europe, Singapore is a dead place. Hongkong is no better. In Batavia it is different. Up to the dinner hour, and after, there is a considerable amount of life and light and animation, and if it be a stretch of the imagination to compare the Noordwijk or the Rizwijk with the Boulevard des Capuchins in Paris, or its open air restaurants with the Cafe de la Paix, it is at least within comparison to say that the resemblance to a Continental town is sufficiently marked to be welcome, while one can have as choice a dinner or supper, with superb wines, in Stamm and Weijns or the Hotel des Indes as in the best restaurants of London and Paris. Not the least noticeable feature of all to the observant visitor will be the punctilio and excellence of the waiting of the Javanese table boys. When one saw the carefulness with which each dish was served, and the superior nature of the side dishes, one thought with a shudder of the sloppy vegetables, the dusty marmalade, and the slipshod waiting of the China boy in some of the hotels it had been our misfortune to patronise in British Colonies.

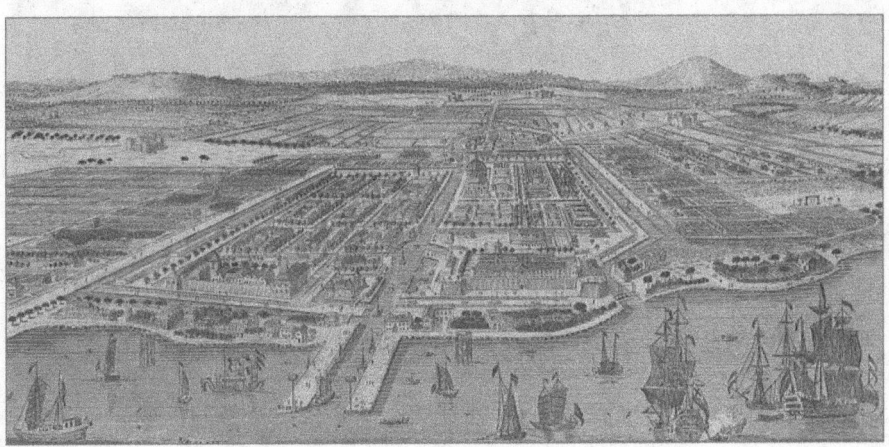

# Pocket Guide for GIs

The United States Army produced a Pocket Guide to Netherlands East Indies in 1945, immediately after the war with Japan ended, to help US troops stationed in the region better understand what was around them and avoid problems with local people. Similar guides were produced for US servicemen in many places around Asia at that time.

The Pocket Guide to the East Indies, *produced by the United States Army for soldiers in the Pacific Theater during World War II*

# All Politeness

*From* Pocket Guide to the East Indies *prepared by the US Army for troops operating in the WWII Pacific Theater*

For the most part they are calm and dignified, finely built, and graceful. Also they are instinctively and sincerely polite. Don't mistake this politeness, especially among the Javanese, for servility; it is just their natural way of showing respect and a part of their everyday character to which they pay a great deal more attention than we do.

*Bathing in the river, c. 1905*

The Indies area is like a huge melting pot where, for thousands of years, different streams of humans have merged, and in turn, spilled over eastward into the farther islands of the Pacific.

*From the US Army* Pocket Guide to the East Indies

# Notoriously Unhealthy

*This is an excerpt from Patrick O'Brian's "The Far Side of the World", one of a series of wonderful novels following the adventures of Captain Jack Aubrey and the doctor/spy Stephen Maturin during the Napoleonic Wars. In this excerpt, the good doctor shares the likely next destination for HMS Surprise with a crewmate.*
'I should be only too happy to sail under your orders, sir,' said Higgins. 'May I ask where the Surprise is bound?'
'That has not yet been publicly given out,' said Stephen. 'But I understand it to be the far side of the world: I have heard mention of Batavia.'
'Oh,' said Higgins, his exultation momentarily checked, for Batavia was most notoriously unhealthy, even worse than the West Indies, where whole ship's companies might die of the yellow jack.

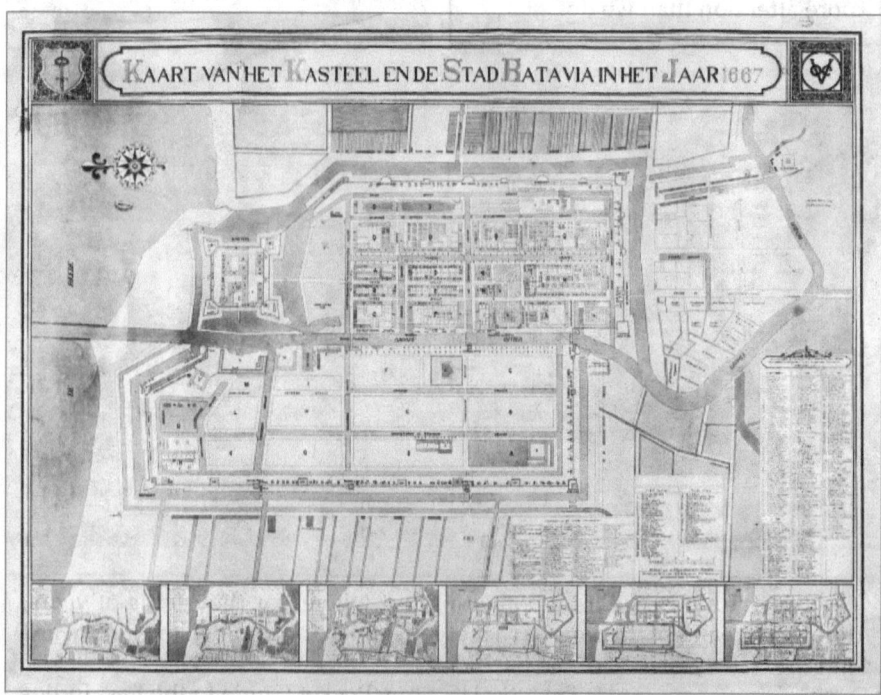

KAART VAN HET KASTEEL EN DE STAD BATAVIA IN HET JAAR 1667

*Batavia 1667. Along the bottom it shows the transformation from Jayakarta 1617 to Batavia 1667*

# The Nine-Planet Federation

*This is the opening to the Philip K. Dick Science fiction novel, Solar Lottery, published in 1955 and set 300 years into the future. It tantalizingly refers to a remarkable future role for Batavia, in the 23rd century.*

There had been harbingers. Early in May of 2203, newsmachines were excited by a flight of white crows over Sweden. A series of unexplained fires demolished half the Oiseau-Lyre Hill, a basic industrial pivot of the system. Small round stones fell near work-camp installations on Mars. At Batavia, the Directorate of the nine-planet Federation, a two-headed Jersey calf was born: a certain sign that something of incredible magnitude was brewing.

17

# The Great Rajah

*Joseph Conrad was one of the great writers of life and doings in the many half-forgotten corners of the world. The Dutch East Indies were well known to him. His book "An Outcast of the Islands" includes this extract:*

BABALATCHI ceased speaking. Lingard shifted his feet a little, uncrossed his arms, and shook his head slowly. The narrative of the events in Sambir, related from the point of view of the astute statesman, the sense of which had been caught here and there by his inattentive ears, had been yet like a thread to guide him out of the sombre labyrinth of his thoughts; and now he had come to the end of it, out of the tangled past into the pressing necessities of the present. With the palms of his hands on his knees, his elbows squared out, he looked down on Babalatchi who sat in a stiff attitude, inexpressive and mute as a talking doll the mechanism of which had at length run down.

"You people did all this," said Lingard at last, "and you will be sorry for it before the dry wind begins to blow again. Abdulla's voice will bring the Dutch rule here."

Babalatchi waved his hand towards the dark doorway.

*Eigen Hulp, a shop at the Molenvliet-West canal, 1890*

*A small coffee plantation in the East Indies in the 19th century.*

"There are forests there. Lakamba rules the land now. Tell me, Tuan, do you think the big trees know the name of the ruler? No. They are born, they grow, they live and they die--yet know not, feel not. It is their land."

"Even a big tree may be killed by a small axe," said Lingard, drily. "And, remember, my one-eyed friend, that axes are made by white hands. You will soon find that out, since you have hoisted the flag of the Dutch."

"Ay--wa!" said Babalatchi, slowly. "It is written that the earth belongs to those who have fair skins and hard but foolish hearts. The farther away is the master, the easier it is for the slave, Tuan! You were too near. Your voice rang in our ears always. Now it is not going to be so. The great Rajah in Batavia is strong, but he may be deceived. He must speak very loud to be heard here. But if we have need to shout, then he must hear the many voices that call for protection. He is but a white man."

"If I ever spoke to Patalolo, like an elder brother, it was for your good--for the good of all," said Lingard with great earnestness.

"This is a white man's talk," exclaimed Babalatchi, with bitter exultation. "I know you. That is how you all talk while you load your guns and sharpen your swords; and when you are ready, then to those who are weak you say: 'Obey me and be happy, or die! You are strange, you white men. You think it is only your wisdom and your virtue and your happiness that are true. You are stronger than the wild beasts, but not so wise. A black tiger knows when he is not hungry--you do not. He knows the difference between himself and those that can speak; you do not understand the difference between yourselves and us--who are men. You are wise and great--and you shall always be fools."

# First Impressions

*The following is a colorful description of Batavia from the collection* Java Facts and Fancies *published in 1905 by Augusta De Wit, the daughter of a Dutch colonial administrator on the island of Sumatra who spent much of her life living in and writing about Batavia.*

My first impression of Java was not that of effulgent light and overpowering magnificence of colour, generally experienced at the first sight of a tropical country; but, on the contrary, of something unspeakably tender, ethereal, and soft. It was in the beginning of the rainy season. Under a sky filmy with diaphanous fleecy texture, in which a tinge of the hidden blue was felt rather than seen, the sea had a pearly sheen, with here and there changefully flickering white lights, and wind-ruffled streaks of a pale violet. The slight haziness in the air somewhat dulled the green of innumerable islets and thickly-wooded reefs, scattered all over the sea; and, blurring their outlines, seemed to lift them until they grew vague and airy as the little clouds of a mackerel sky, wafted hither and thither by the faintest wind. In the distance the block of square white buildings on the landing-place – pointed out as the railway station and the custom houses – stood softly outlined against a background of whitish-grey sky and mist-blurred trees.

Slowly the steamer glided on. And, as we now approached the roadstead of Batavia, there came swimming towards the ship numbers of native boats, darting out from between the islets, and diving up out of the shadows along the wooded shore, like so many waterfowl. Swiftest of all were the "praos'" very slight hulls, almost disappearing under their one immense whitish-brown sail, shaped like

*Praos boats on the river, c. 1905*

20

*Jakarta Bay, Batavia*

a bird's wing, and thrown back with just the same impatient fling—ready for a swoop and rake—so exactly resembling sea-gulls skimming along, as to render the comparison almost a description. On they came, drawing purplish furrows through the pearly greys and whites of the sea. And, in their wake, darting hither and thither with the jerky movements of water-spiders, quite a swarm of little black canoes—hollowed-out tree-trunks, kept in balance by bamboo outriggers, which spread on either side like sprawling, scurrying legs. As they approached, we saw that the boats were piled with many-tinted fruit, above which the naked bodies of the oarsmen rose, brown and shiny, and the wet paddle gleamed in its leisurely-seeming dip and rise, which yet sent the small skiff bounding onward. They were alongside soon, and the natives clambered on board, laden with fragrant wares. They did not take the trouble of hawking them about, agile as they had

proved themselves, but calmly squatted down amid their piled-up baskets of yellow, scarlet, crimson, and orange fruit—a medley of colours almost barbaric in its magnificence, notwithstanding the soberer tints of blackening purple, and cool, reposeful green; and calmly awaited customers. Under the gaudy kerchiefs picturesquely framing the dark brows, their brown eyes had that look of thoughtful—or is it all thoughtless?—content, which we of the North know only in the eyes of babies, crooning in their mother's lap. And, as they answered our questions, their speech had something childlike too, with its soft consonants and clear vowels, long-drawn-out on a musical modulation, that glided all up and down the gamut. They had a great charm for me, their flatness of features and meagreness of limbs notwithstanding; and I thought, that, if not quite the fairies, they might well be the "brownies" of that enchanted garden that men call Java.

# A Nation In The Making

Only slowly is a common feeling of being Indonesian spreading among the mass of the people. As it does so, however, it arouses a keen sense of pride and patriotism. The Indonesians may well be looked upon as a people and a nation in the making.

*From the US Army* Pocket Guide to the East Indies

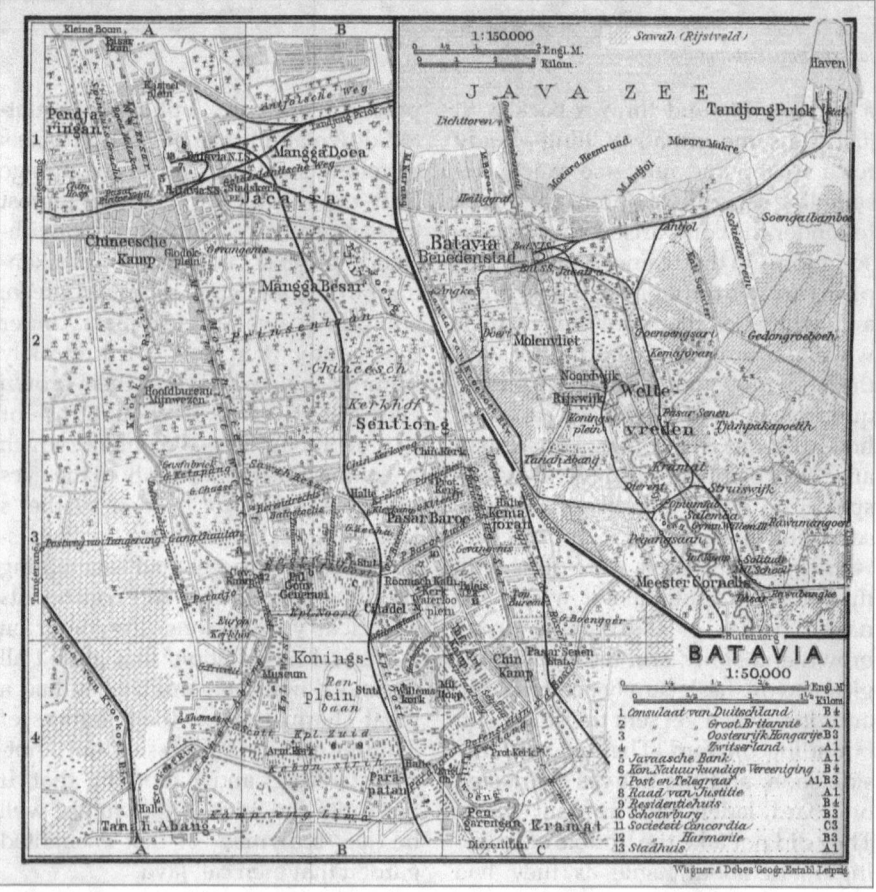

# The Amboyna Massacre

The Portuguese were the first to enter the spice trade in the East Indies; however, they were soon ousted by the English and by the Dutch. By 1605, the Dutch East India Company had conquered the Portuguese center of trade, Amboyna on Ambon Island, and begun their quest to create a monopoly on the spice trade, causing tensions with the English East India Company. The friction between the two companies unavoidably got the national governments involved and in 1619 the warring parties signed a Treaty of Defence meant to facilitate cooperation in the East Indies. Cooperation did not necessarily occur, however, as the parties stoked suspicions and filed grievances against each other. Then, in 1623, Dutch suspicions of the English at Amboyna became concrete whena Japanese mercenary was caught spying. Under torture, the soldier admitted to a conspiracy to seize the fortress and assassinate the governor and implicated the captain of the English on the island as being involved. The Dutch-then rounded up and arrested all the English personnel, questioning them, most often through the torture of waterboarding. The suspects eventually confessed to the conspiracy and were sentenced to death, though six were eventually pardoned.

The Dutch authorities at Amboyna executed 20 men, 10 of whom were Englishmen, and beheaded the English captain and impaled his head on a pole for all to see. Following the executions, those that were pardoned went first to Batavia to complain to the governor-general and, when they were unable to obtain justice, sailed with the rest of the English from Batavia to England. The story of Amboyna caused uproar in England and the Dutch East India Company eventually tried those in charge of the torture, though they were all acquitted.

The manner of Torturing & Executing the English and Japonese At Amboyna, and the Oran-keys and Nobles of Poloroone :—
Sutton Nicholls sculp.

23

# Port of Tandjong Priok

*A description of a visitor's arrival in Tandjong Priok, the main port for the city of Batavia, by Thomas H. Reid published in 1908 in* Across the Equator, A Holiday Trip in Java.

The visitor landing at Tandjong Priok, the port of Batavia, after his experience of other Far Eastern ports, cannot fail to be struck by the excellence of the arrangements for berthing vessels and for storing cargo. We British people are so accustomed to the idea that our ports are the best and our trading arrangements unequalled that we are astonished when we discover that our shipping and commercial rivals know how to do some things better than ourselves, and that all wisdom is not to be found within the confines of England and among the people who are proud to own it as their place of birth. Our Far Eastern ports owe their supremacy to geographical position almost entirely. We have realised that during recent years in Singapore, and in our haste to correct the

*Port of Tanjung Priok, in the 1940s*

mistakes of former officials and residents, the Straits Settlements paid rather heavily when they expropriated the Tanjong Pagar Company which owned the wharves, docks and warehouses. Tandjong Priok may not handle the shipping that Tanjong Pagar does, but if they were called upon to do so, we have not the least doubt that our Dutch neighbours would rise readily to the occasion.

There is a Customs examination at Tandjong Priok. In our own case, it was a mere formality, the new duty on imported cameras not applying to our well-used kodak, since it was being taken out of the country again. But we could not help contrasting to the disadvantage of Singapore the examination of Chinese and other Asiatic passengers. Theoretically, in Singapore, there is no Customs service. It is a free port, and so, theoretically, one may land there free of vexatious examinations, such as one experiences at some Continental ports or on the wharves at San Francisco. But, as a matter of fact, they who have occasion to walk along the sea front in Singapore may see Asiatic passengers at any of the landing places turning out their baggage in sun or rain, while chentings — the hirelings of the rich Chinese Syndicate which "farms" or leases the opium and spirit monopolies — examine it for opium or spirits. There is no proper landing place, absolutely no proper arrangements for overhauling baggage, with the result that these poor Asiatics are subjected to examination under conditions that are a disgrace to a place which arrogates a front place in the seaports of the world. They do things better at Tandjong Priok.

*The Port of Tandjong Priok, Batavia's main port, in the 1930s*

# Meeting the Javians

*Captain William Dampier was an English explorer who, among other things, was the first to explore much of Australia. In 1699, he traveled to Batavia and the following is his account of meeting the Javanese people as recorded in his diary later published as* A Continuation of a Voyage to New Holland.

In the afternoon before we had seen many proas; but none came off to us; and in the night we saw many fires ashore. This day a large proa came aboard of us, and lay by our side an hour. There were only 4 men in her, all Javians, who spoke the Malayan language. They asked if we were English; I answered we were; and presently one of them came aboard and presented me with a small hen, some eggs and coconuts; for which I gave some beads and a small look-ing-glass, and some glass bottles. They also gave me some sugarcane, which I distributed to such of my men as were scorbutic. They told me there were 3 English ships at Batavia.

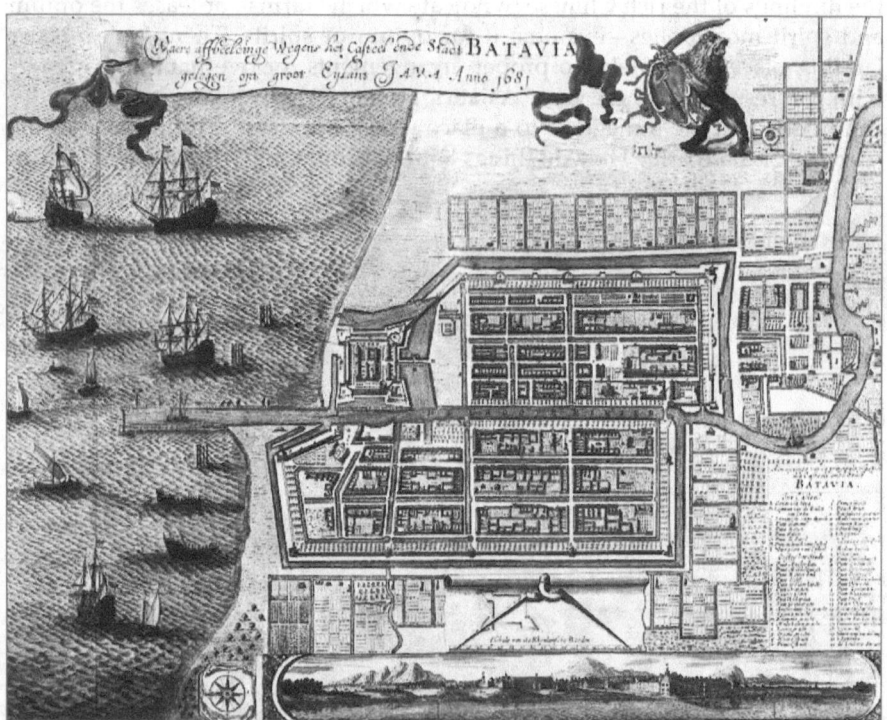

*Castle at Batavia, 1681*

# A Cup of Java

Coffee was first brought to the island of Java by the Dutch who were looking for a substitute for the slowly dwindling spice trade. By 1719, the Dutch East Indies had taken over as the primary supplier of coffee to Europe. In fact, Europe drank so much of the East Indies coffee that the name "Java", the island where the coffee plantations were built, continues to be a word used to refer to coffee even today.

*The Java computer programming language, released in 1995, was given its name from the large quantities of Java coffee consumed by the creators of the program.*

*A coffee factory where the beans are dried and roasted*

*One of the gates into Batavia.*

# From Singapore to Batavia

*From* Across the Equator A Holiday Trip in Java *by Thomas H. Reid, 1908*
The voyage across the Equator from Singapore is a smooth one, for the most part through narrow straits and seldom out of sight of islands clad with verdure down to the water's edge. As our steamer pounded her way out of Singapore Harbour in the early morning, islands appeared to spring out of the sea, and seascape after seascape followed in rapid succession, suggesting the old-fashioned panoramic pictures of childhood's acquaintance. One's idea of scenery, after all, is more or less a matter of comparison. One passenger compares the scene with the Kyles of Bute; another with the Inland Sea of Japan, at the other end of the world. Yet, this tropical waterway is unlike either, and has a characteristic individuality of its own, none the less charming because of the comparisons it suggests and the associations it recalls.

*Commercial district in Batavia, c. 1905*

# Waterboarding

The Dutch administrators of the Netherlands East Indies were noted for the ferocity of their administration methods. Waterboarding, a torture technique, involving dousing the victim or prisoner with huge amounts of water, was a very common method of investigation used by the Dutch in Batavia particularly in the 17th century. In contrast to the methods of waterboarding we now understand were used in the US War of Terror after 9.11, the Dutch method consisted of wrapping a cloth around the head of the victim onto which was poured large and constant amounts of water until the cloth was fully soaked and the victim could not breathe without sucking in water. This caused an experience akin to that of drowning. The body of the victim was reported to swell up to gargantuan proportions due to the ingestion of huge amounts of water.

*Depictions from the 18th century of water torure and waterboarding as carried out constantly by the Dutch authorities against victims and prisoners as a means to extract confessions.*

*The Condition of the English in the Dungeon, and their Execution*

*A postcard depicting life in Batavia*

# Old and New

*A description of Batavia from* On the Equator *by Harry de Windt, a prolific travel writer and the brother-in-law of the English ruler, James Brooke, of the kingdom of Sarawak on the island of Borneo*

The lower part of the town, or, as it is called, Old Batavia, consists entirely of warehouses, go-downs, and native houses. No Europeans can live here, so unhealthy is it, nor can even one night be passed in this quarter with impunity. The upper town—which is named Weltereoden, "well content"—consists of Government House and the houses of all the officials and merchants in Batavia. Most of these houses are situated around the "Koenig's Plein," a large grass plain some 1,000 yards in circumference, which in the time of the English occupation was used as a racecourse. On one side of this stands the governor's palace, a large stone building of modern architecture, while on the other side of the plain is a statue of the Netherland lion.

*Weltevreden*

Grand Hotel: „Java", Weltevreden
Leeskamer

# A Portrait of Batavia

*W. Basil Worsfold, an English scholar and writer most known for his work on South Africa, describes the city of Batavia in his work* A Visit to Java *published in 1893*

Batavia may be divided into three parts. First, there is the business quarter, the oldest, where the houses are tall and built in the style still prevalent in the warm countries of Europe, with balconies and verandahs and widely projecting eaves, and where the streets are narrow. Then there is the Chinese Campong, which, with the adjacent streets, occupies the central portion of the town, containing the bulk of the population closely packed in their curious dwellings. And, lastly, there is Weltevreden, the Dutch town, where the officials, the military, and the merchants reside.

All three quarters are possessed of a separate beauty. The elaborately carved pediments and ponderous doors, the heavy balconies and eaves of the houses, give an old-world quaintness to the first, which is enhanced by the crowd of many-shaped and variously coloured boats that line the quays that front the offices on either side of the Great River. Nothing could be more delightful than the setting of the red-tiled roofs, with their dragon-decorated ridges and parapets, on the wooden trellis fronts and canvas blinds of the Chinese houses. Weltevreden, too, is not without attractions. The broad porticoes of dazzling white, with their Ionic columns and marble floors, are often set in a fair surrounding of green trees. The compounds and gardens are always verdant, and sometimes radiant with bright-leaved shrubs and flowers. Especially the broad green-covered squares and the wide roads arched with noble trees speak of coolness and repose in a hot and weary land. On the outskirts of the town, along the country roads, where the cocoa palm and banana plantations begin, are the bamboo cottages of the Sundanese natives.

*The governor's palace*

35

# The Hotel Des Indes

Hotel des Indes was first opened in Batavia in 1829 and until it finally closed in 1971, it was one of the most renowned hostelries in Asia. An endless succession of famous patrons stayed there. It was THE place to stay when one listed batavia. When first opened by a French hotelier, it was named 'Hotel de Provence', and was briefly Hotel Rotterdam before changing to the name that made it famous. After Indonesian independence, it was renamed 'Hotel Duta Indonesia', but it was finally demolished to make way for a shopping mall. Ocean travelers in the 19th century arriving in the port of Batavia were taken to shore with small boats and dropped off at the 'Kleine Boom' customs office. They were then taken to 'Hotel Des Indes' in a carriage along Molenvliet street. In 1958, the hotel was still welcoming people such as American actor John Wayne. Nevertheless the hotel's commercial decline had begun, especially after 1962 when the competing 'Hotel Indonesia' was opened. The grand old 'Hotel Des Indes' was demolished to make way for the shopping mall 'Duta Merlin'.

> The Hotel de Nederlanden is a huge building with any amount of dependencies, in front of which run long, wide verandahs. My bedroom was in one of these, and my sitting-room in the verandah in front of it.
> *From Scented Isles and Coral Gardens by C.D. Mackellar, 1912*

## THE HOTEL DES INDES
### WELTEVREDEN (BATAVIA) JAVA

—

Cable address:

„INDES" WELTEVREDEN

✛

*To foreigners the attraction of this Hotel is mainly its extensive pavilion system (private bungalows, one of which is portrayed in the next photograph) which one has been able to apply on account of the extensive grounds (occupying over 16 acres) belonging to the hotel*

Codes:
| *Mercuur 3rd. ed.* |
| *A. B. C. 5th. „* |
| *A. B. C. 6th. „* |
| *Bentley* |

### THE HOTEL DES INDES
WELTEVREDEN (BATAVIA) JAVA

+

*Special Dinner – Music – Dancing.*
*The accomodation as well as the*
*cuisine are unsurpassed in Java*

*The main dining saloon*
*with over 500 seats*

# The Big Durian

*The durian fruit, from where modern Jakarta (Batavia) gets its nickname, is a known for its strong odor. The following excerpts from W. Basil Worsfold in A Visit to Java in 1893 and C.D. Mackellar in Scented Isles and Coral Gardens in 1912 describe the fruit*

The durian is as large as a cocoa-nut, and its exterior is armed with spikes; the fruit is soft and pulpy, tasting like a custard in flavour, but it has a horrible smell, and possesses strong laxative qualities. Mr. Wallace devotes several pages to a description of its various qualities, remarking that "to eat durians is a new sensation, worth a voyage to the East to experience."

Then he explains that this much-prized fruit, a large thing with a hard rind, is perfectly delightful and beloved by every one, only that it has this awful smell. At first you cannot go near it — I can well believe that — and when you do, it is long ere you have the courage to attack it. You generally give it up at first and fly from it, but once you overcome the smell, and taste the fruit, you are content. Perhaps so.

## NO DURIAN

The "No Durian" sign that can often be found next to "No Smoking" signs due to the fruit's strong odor.

The durian fruit is most known for its strong, horrible smell.

# This Awful Smell

"It is a most interesting and beautiful place," I say, "but it must be un-healthy with such terrific drainage — or want of drainage."

"Drainage ?" queries Carel.

"Yes, this awful smell that pervades the whole place — how can you endure it ?"

Carel leaned back in his chair and laughed till he was no longer pale, but quite rosy.

"It is not drains," he said, "it is the durian — our famous fruit!"

*From Scented Isles and Coral Gardens by C.D. Mackellar, 1912*

*Huntley & Palmers Biscuits*

# The Betawi

The Dutch East Indies, and Batavia in particular, was the center of trade in Asia for close to 200 years. The prosperity and economic importance of the city brought together many different ethnic groups including Malay, Portuguese, Arab, Chinese, Indian, and Dutch. The descendants from the mixing of all of these groups within Batavia are known as the Betawi people. The name Betawi is derived from the name Batavia, the city around which most of the population lives. They are largely Muslim, however there is a small group of Christians descended from the Portuguese. The customs and culture of the Betawi is a collection of European, Chinese, Arabic, and local traditions, a mix noticeable in the Betawi dialect which has many loan words from the languages.

*Sundanese boys playing the Angklung, a traditional instrument made of bamboo that creates a resonant sound when struck, 1918*

*Betawi dancers and musicians*

*A Javanese priyayi woman and her servants, 1865. The priyayi were the noble class in Javanese society.*

# Nightlife in Batavia

*Thomas H. Reid, a traveler to Batavia in September 1907, writes about the hotels and nightlife of the city in Across the Equator,* A Holiday Trip in Java, *published the year following his trip.*

Batavia is favoured in that it has a choice of several good hotels. Whoever selects the Hotel Nederland or the Hotel des Indes will say that the other "best Hotels in the Far East" have something yet to learn in the accommodation of visitors, general cleanliness, and moderation of prices. After sundown, so far as Europeans are concerned, with the exception of the little life seen under the electric light of Raffles Hotel and the Hotel de l'Europe, Singapore is a dead place. Hongkong is no better. In Batavia it is different. Up to the dinner hour, and after, there is a considerable amount of life and light and animation, and if it be a stretch of the imagination to compare the Noordwijk or the Rizwijk with the Boulevard des Capuchins in Paris, or its open air restaurants with the Cafe de la Paix, it is at least within comparison to say that the resemblance to a Continental town is sufficiently marked to be welcome, while one can have as choice a dinner or supper, with superb wines, in Stamm and Weijns or the Hotel des Indes as in the best restaurants of London and Paris. Not the least noticeable feature of all to the observant visitor will be the punctilio and excellence of the waiting of the Javanese table boys. When one saw the carefulness with which each dish was served, and the superior nature of the side dishes, one thought with a shudder of the sloppy vegetables, the dusty marmalade, and the slipshod waiting of the China boy in some of the hotels it had been our misfortune to patronise in British Colonies.

# Gaming & Gambling in Sumatra

*William Marsden was a civil servant with the English East India Company and wrote most extensively on the Malaysian language. The following description of the vices of the East Indies is from his work* The History of Sumatra *published in 1811*

Through every rank of the people there prevails a strong spirit of gaming, which is a vice that readily insinuates itself into minds naturally indisposed to the avocations of industry; and, being in general a sedentary occupation, is more adapted to a warm climate, where bodily exertion is in few instances considered as an amusement.

Dice: Beside the common species of gambling with dice, they have several others; as the judi, a mode of playing with small shells, which are taken up by handfuls, and, being counted out by a given number at a time (generally that of the party engaged), the success is determined by the fractional number remaining, the amount of which is previously guessed at by each of the party.

Cock-Fighting: To cock-fighting they are still more passionately addicted, and it is indulged to them under certain regulations. Where they are perfectly independent their propensity to it is so great that it resembles rather a serious occupation than a sport. You seldom meet a man travelling in the country without a cock under his arm, and sometimes fifty persons in a company when there is a bimbang in one of the neighbouring villages. They often game high at their meetings; particularly when a superstitious faith in the invincibility of their bird has been strengthened by past success. A hundred Spanish dollars is no very uncommon risk, and instances have occurred of a father's staking his children or wife, and a son his mother or sisters, on the issue of a battle, when a run of ill luck has stripped them of property and rendered them desperate. Quarrels, attended with dreadful consequences, have often arisen on these occasions.

Opium: The Sumatrans, and more particularly the Malays, are much attached, in common with many other eastern people, to the custom of smoking opium. The poppy which produces it not growing on the island, it is annually imported from Bengal in considerable quantities, in chests containing a hundred and forty pounds each. It is made up in cakes of five or six pounds weight, and packed with dried leaves; in which situation it will continue good and vendible for two years, but after that period grows hard and diminishes considerably in value. It is of a darker colour, and is supposed to have less strength than the Turkey opium. About a hundred and fifty chests are consumed annually on the west coast of Sumatra, where it is purchased, on an average, at three hundred dollars the chest, and sold again in smaller quantities at five or six. But on occasions of extraordinary scarcity I have known it to sell for its weight in silver, and a single chest to fetch upwards of three thousand dollars.

*An opium factory in the Dutch East Indies*

*Defences around Batavia in the 1660s*

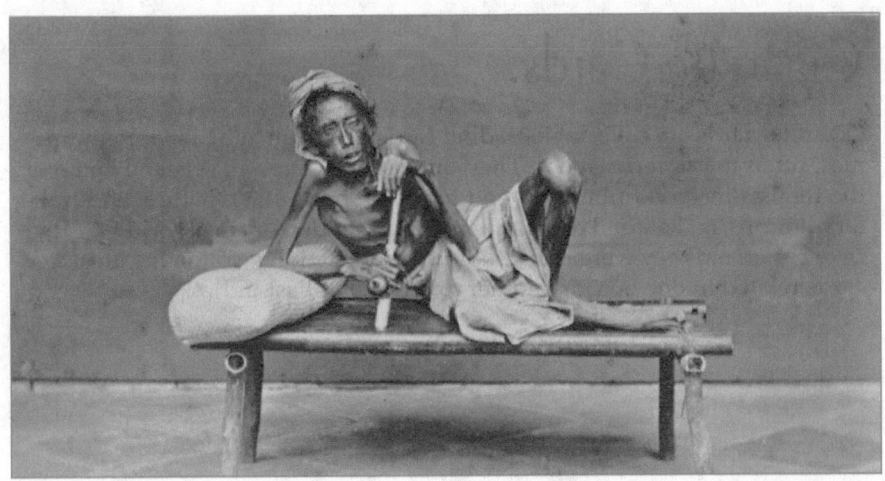

*Opium addicts on Java around 1900*

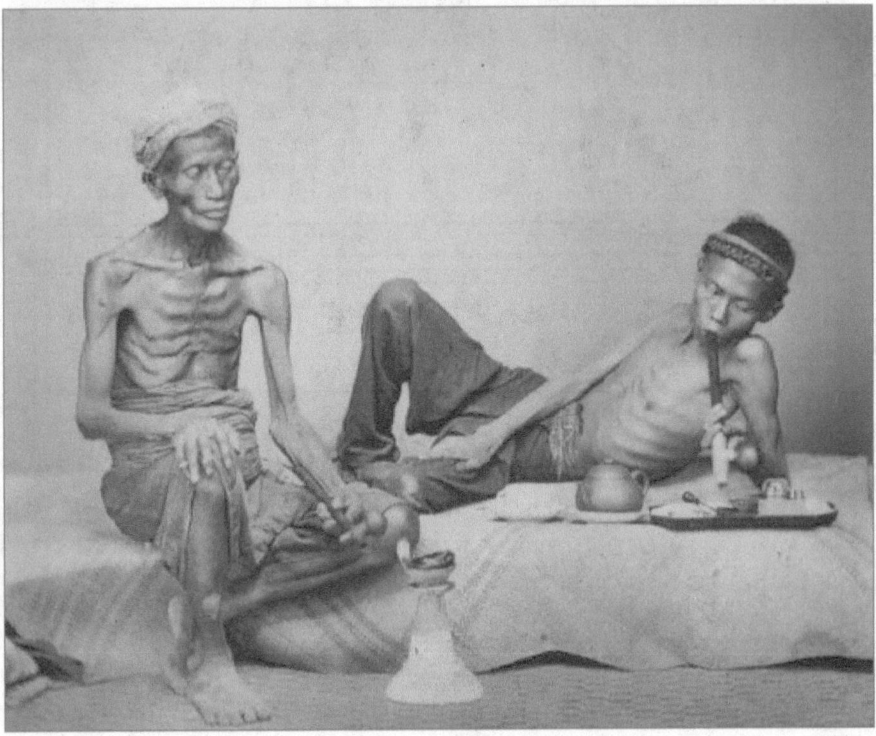

# Cigarette Cards

Cigarette cards are collectable trading cards once issued by tobacco companies, often for advertisement. They often were issued in sets and some of the themes included film stars and models, sports stars, nature, and military uniforms. The trend of printing the cards ended during World War II to save paper and they were never fully reintroduced. The following are a few cards related in one way or another to the Dutch East Indies.

48

FRANKLYN'S CIGARETTES.

JAVA.

CHILDREN OF ALL NATIONS

A SERIES OF 50

24

JAVA.

One of the islands of the Dutch East Indies, Java is a land of wonderful beauty and fertility where the cultivation of rice has been brought to perfection, several crops being harvested during the year. The sturdy lightly-clothed Javanese children may be seen playing in the rice-fields while their parents are busy planting or harvesting the crop. The babies are carried by their mothers on the left hip, in a kind of cradle of cloth hung from the right shoulder.

PUSH

FRANKLYN, DAVEY & CO.
BRANCH OF THE IMPERIAL TOBACCO CO.
(OF GREAT BRITAIN & IRELAND), LTD.

LAMBERT & BUTLER'S CIGARETTES

FISHING BOATS AT BATAVIA, NETHERLANDS INDIES

49

# Kite Games

*From Java Facts and Fancies by Augusta De Wit, 1905*

During the East monsoon, when high south-easterly winds may be counted upon, flying kites is a favorite game; and not only with boys, but with grown men. Groups of them may often be seen in the squares and parks of Batavia or in the fields near the town, floating large kites, shaped like birds and winged dragons, which, in ascending, emit a whistling sound, clear and plaintive as that of a wind-harp. They sometimes remain soaring for days together, and strains of that aerial music, attuned in sad "minore," float out upon every passing breath of air. Passers-by in the street look up, shading their eyes from the sun, at the bright things soaring and singing in the sky, and dispute much about the melodious merits of each. The paper singing-birds, called "swangan," are very popular with the masses. But the true amateurs of the sport prefer another kind, the "palembang" and "koenchier" kites, which do not sing but fight, or, at least, in skilful hands, can be made to fight. These are made of Chinese paper, and decorated with the image of some god or hero of Javanese mythology. The cord twisted out of strong rameh fibre is coated with a paste of pounded glass or earthenware, mixed with starch. This renders it strong and cutting as steel wire. The aim of each player is to make the cord of his kite, when up

*Weltevreden Palace at the Koningsplein square, 1880*

in the air, cross his opponent's cord, and then, with a swift downward pull, cut it in two: a manœuvre which requires considerable dexterity. The game is played according to strict rules and with some degree of ceremony and etiquette, as prescribed by the "adat" – the immemorial law of courtesy which, in Java, regulates all things, from matters of life and death down to the arrangement of a girl's scarf and the games which children play. When all the kites are well up in the air, tugging on the strained cords, each player chooses his antagonist. He advances to within a few paces, makes his kite approach the other's, all but touch it, swerve, and come back; having thus preferred his challenge, he retires to the place first occupied. Thither, presently, his opponent follows him, and, by the exact repetition of his manœuvre, signifies his acceptance of the combat, retiring afterwards in the same stately manner. Then the contest begins. The agile figures of the players dart hither and thither, fitfully, with swift impulse and sudden pause, and abrupt swerve, bending this way and that, swaying, with head thrown back and right arm flung up along the straining cord. The groups of spectators, standing well aside so as not to interfere with the movements of the players, gaze upward with bated breath. And, aloft, sparkling with purple and gold, their long streamers spread out upon the wind, the two kites soar and swoop, swerve, plunge a second time, slowly swim upwards again, glide a

little further, and hang motionless. The thin cords are all but invisible; the fantastic shapes high in the air seem animated with a life of their own, wilful, untiring, eager to pursue, and swift to escape, full of feints and ruses. Suddenly, as one again plunges, the other, tranquilly sailing aloft, trembles, staggers, tumbles over, and leaping up, scuds down the wind and is gone. The severed length of cord comes down with a thud; and, as the unlucky owner darts away after the fugitive, in the forlorn hope of finding it hanging somewhere in the branches of a tree, the victor lets his kite reascend and triumphantly hover aloft, straining against the wind, and tugging upon the strong shiny cord that has come off scathless from the encounter.

*A family photo*

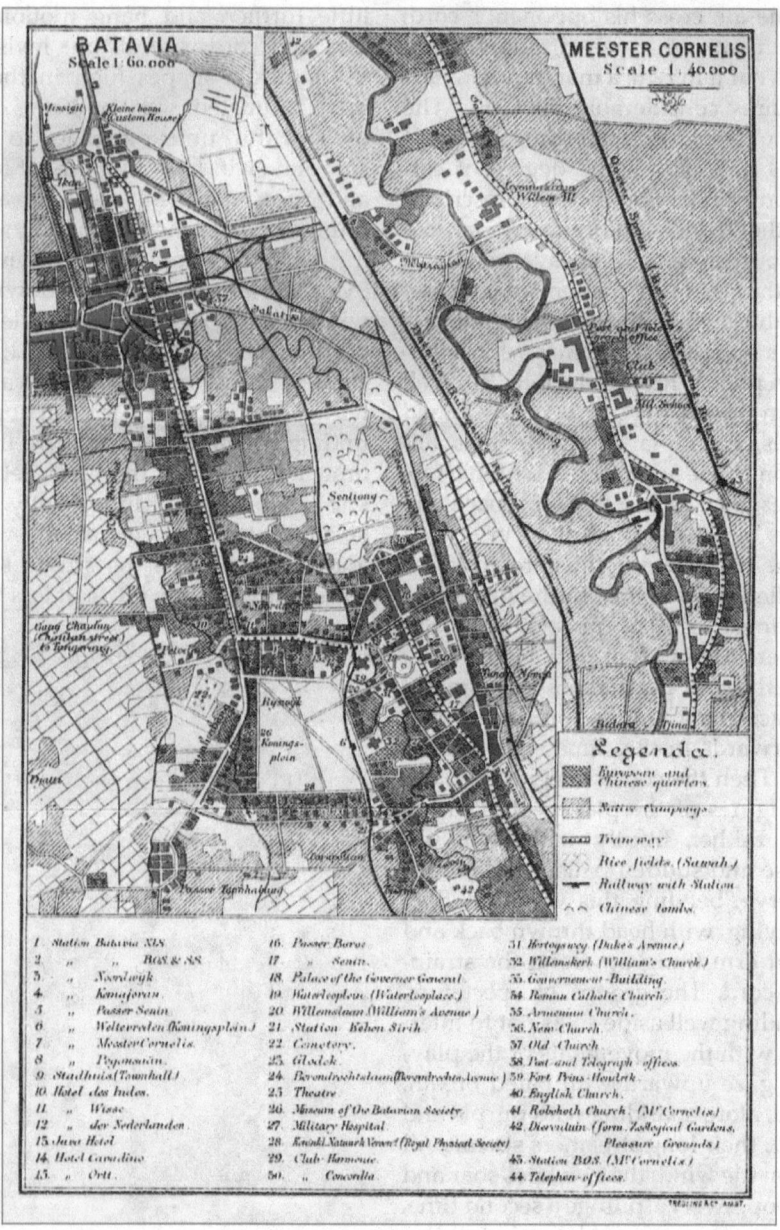

*Map of the neighborhoods of Batavia c. 1897*

# Rice Table

Feasting was a part of the East Indies culture that the Dutch colonists embraced enthusiastically. The rijsttafel, or rice table, was one such colonial feast started by the Dutch. The festive meal would begin by placing a large platter of rice at the center of the table and surrounding it with anywhere from 7 to 60 – 40 was the most common – small bowls of side dishes. These side dishes included foods from all over the Dutch East Indies as well as hybrid Chinese-Indonesian or European-Indonesian dishes. The popularity of the rijsttafel allowed the Dutch colonialists to enjoy a varied range of dishes in one meal but to impress visitors with the richness of their colony. At the height of colonial success, one of the most talked about rijsttafel was served at the Hotel des Indes in Batavia for Sunday luncheon. Today, however, you are more likely to find rijsttafel in the Netherlands than in Indonesia, where it is only served in a few fine-dining restaurants.

# A Never-ending Feast

*An experience at a Batavian rice-table feast as described by Augusta de Wit in* Java Facts and Fancies, *1905.*

And, last not least, the meal itself is such as never was tasted on sea or land before. The principal dish is rice and chicken, which sounds simple enough. But on this as a basis an entire system of things inedible has been constructed: besides fish, flesh, and fricassees, all manner of curries, sauces, pickles, preserved fruit, salt eggs, fried bananas, "sambals" of fowl's liver, fish-roe, young palm-shoots, and the gods of Javanese cookery alone know what more, all strongly spiced, and sprinkled with cayenne. There is nothing under the sun but it may be made into a sambal; and a conscientious cook would count that a lost day on which he had not sent in at the very least twenty of such nondescript dishes to the table of his master, for whose digestion let all gentle souls pray! And, when to all this I have added that these many and strange things must be eaten with a spoon in the right hand and a fork in the left, the reader will be able to judge how very complicated an affair the rice-table is, and how easily the uninitiated may come to grief over it. For myself, I shall never forget my first experience of the thing. I had just come in from a ride through the town, and I suppose the glaring sunlight, the strangely-accoutred crowd, the novel sights and sounds of the city must have slightly gone to my head (there are plenty of intoxicants besides "gin" vide the Autocrat of the Breakfast Table). Anyhow,

I entered the "back gallery" with a sort of "here-the-conquering-hero-comes" feeling; looked at the long table groaning under its dozens of rice-bowls, scores of dishes of fowls and fish, and hundreds of sambal-saucers, arrayed between pyramids of bananas, mangosteens, and pine-apples, as if I could have eaten it all by way of "apéritif;" sat me down; heaped my plate up with everything that came my way; and fell to. What followed I have no words to express. Suffice it to say, that in less time than I now take to relate it, I was reduced to the most abject misery — my lips smarting with the fiery touch of the sambal; my throat the more sorely scorched for the hasty draught of water with which, in my ignorance, I had tried to allay the intolerable heat; and my eyes full of tears, which it was all I could do to prevent from openly gushing down my cheeks, in streams of utter misery. A charitable person advised me to put a little salt on my tongue, (as children are told to do on the tail of the bird they want to catch). I did so; and, after a minute of the most excruciating torture, the agony subsided. I gasped, and found I was still alive. But there and then I vowed to myself I would never so much as look at a rice-table again.

*A rice table at the Hotel des Indes*

# Boomerang Effect

*In an article published in the year 2000, the excellent newspaper* Jakarta Post
*celebrated the schools left behind from the period of Dutch rule.*

In the early days, Dutch schools in Jakarta were once dubbed as the most prestigious in the country. At that time, only children of ruling colonial masters and the wealthy pribumi (local residents) were allowed to study at these colonial schools. If you have any doubts about this fact, just ask your grandmother or grandfather. They might not only tell you about how Indonesian children struggled for the opportunity to learn there but may also continue to relive their memories by telling you more about this historical period. Four of the five buildings,

*Students of HIS with paternal figure in 1934*

most of which have faced several renovations,are located in Central Jakarta. They are the SMPN I junior high school in Cikini, STM I techni-
cal high school on Jl. Budi Utomo in Sawah Besar area, nearby SMUN
I senior high school and SMKK Negeri Jakarta vocational high school
on Jl. Sutomo. The other building is on Jl. Manggarai Utara I in South
Jakarta and is now the SDN 01 Manggarai Utara elementary school.
The five buildings, now all run by the state, were mostly designed using Indische architecture with high ceiling and wide windows to beat
the tropical climate. The 91-year-old Cikini school building was originally the prominent Hollandsch Inlandsche School (HIS elementary
school) and also for students of the Meer Uitgebreide Lagere Onder-
wijs (MULO junior high school). Built in 1909, the building still has
its original high roof and extra wide windows in its classrooms. Those
who once had the privileged opportunity to attend lessons in these
classrooms would instantly be taken back in time to their childhood.
The same atmosphere also exists in the SMUN I building, which used
to be the Algemeene Middelbare School (AMS). It would have been
equal to a senior high school today. Built in 1930, the construction of
the building remains solidly intact with its broad corridors. A court-
yard in the middle of the building is still used for sport activities as it
was in its former days. At one time, the AMS building was once used
as the headquarters of the Indonesian Navy (BKR Laut Pusat), before
being occupied again by Dutch soldiers (NICA). A few years after independence was granted in 1945, the building was the state-owned
SMUN I school, also known as SMUN I Budi Utomo.

SMKK Negeri Jakarta was constructed in 1932 and used to be the
Europeesch Lagere School (ELS), an elementary school for Dutch children. Another protected school building, SDN 01 Manggarai Utara in
South Jakarta, used to provide classes only for children of top officials
of the Dutch Staat Spoorwegen railway company since the school was
constructed in their housing complex. Built in 1916, the building was
originally called Marschalk Land. The roof was built with another di-
rectly above, both at the same degree of angle. The small space in between allowed a continuous flow of air to ventilate the rooms below.

Education expert J. Drost said the Dutch colonials started to intro-
duce the formal schools here simply because they "needed people to
work at the colonial service". Previously, the school system was initially in the form of religious institutions, such as pesantren (Islamic
boarding schools) and those run by the Dutch Christian missionaries.
But the education had a boomerang effect on the colonials as through
the Dutch schools, intellectual Indonesian nationalists were born.

# Menteng

In the 1910s, with Batavia growing and the economy strong, the Duitch administrators decided it was tiome to expand the city and build a new residential district primarily for themselves, using the best town planning and tropical villa construction principles then known. The result was Menteng, originall called Nieuw Gondangdia. It is located just to the south of the old town center. In recent decades, Menteng has been the residence of choice of many senior Indonesian officials, and the President of the United States Barack Obama spent his youth here, attending local schools including St. Francis of Assisi School. The district was developed by a Dutch real estate company N.V. de Bouwploeg, founded by Pieter Adriaan Jacobus Moojen. A 1975 decree declared Menteng to be a cultural heritage area due to the distinctive architecture of its residences.

*The headquarters of N.V. de Bouwploeg in the 1930s, now the Cut Mutiah mosque.*

# Utopian Garden City

*An excerpt from the book Planning the Megacity: Jakarta in the Twentieth Century, by Christopher Silver and published in 2008, discussing the origins and significance of the Menteng project.*

The prestige of Menteng within the context of colonial Batavia would eventually be transferred to the indigenous urban elite of Jakarta in the post-colonial period. Whereas many emblems of the colonial past were shunned, Menteng as a neighbourhood of prestige persisted. It provided a residential anchor for the central core of the city that remarkably withstood the pressures of commercial encroachment in later years. This should be attributed, in good measure, to the quality of the community's original plan, which effectively incorporated elements of interconnectedness with adjacent areas while preserving the area's spatial integrity through an ingenious system of streets and boulevards and contiguous structures that conformed to the system.

The initial development of Menteng took place between 1910 and 1918, based on a plan by Dutch architect, P.A. Mooijen . . . . Mooijen's original plan bore a striking resemblance to the [utopian] garden city model of the English reformer Ebenezer Howard, in that it combined wide cross-cutting boulevards with concentric rings of streets and a central public square. . . . Although Menteng was originally intended to be an exclusive community, there were, in fact, many modest houses built along its edges, perhaps to serve as a buffer, but also ensuring occupancy by a cross section of the European community of Batavia.

Not only in size but also in style, Menteng was the most important neighborhood in the city and introduced into the urban landscape a diversity of traditional and modern structures that changed and enhanced the look of the city. Traditional Indisch style one-storey villas were intermingled with two-storey structures. There were three types of small villas, the Tosari, the Sumenep, and the Madura, all of which were designed with facilities to accommodate automobiles and hosue servants but were kept under 500 square metres. There was a sprinkling of Art Deco style houses and also innovative roof designs, including widespread use of the mansard roof.

Although escalating city centre land values exerted pressures on the edges of Menteng to convert to more convert to more intensive non-residential uses in later years, the core of the community became the focus of preservationists and re-greening advocates in the 1990s. The community plan of Menteng, and the lifestyle that it was intended to provide, endured as the city around it changed drastically.

# Speaking in Tongues

When the Dutch East India Company arrived in Indonesia, they adopted the Malay language, already popular in trade and politics, as the administrative language of trade and of their trading center, Batavia. And so, through trade, the Malay on Java began to change and absorb pieces of the Dutch language and dominant local languages, most importantly Javanese and Sundanese. Eventually the Indonesian language was formed from the mix of Malay and other languages, locally known as Bahasa Indonesia. Today, Indonesian is the official language, following the declaration of independence in 1945, and is still most widely used as a language of trade and administration. Most people speak it as a second language as there are still more than 700 languages spoken throughout the country; Javanese and Sundanese remain the most widely spoken mother tongues throughout most of Indonesia. However, in the area of Batavia, now Jakarta, Malay is most dominant, a trait leftover from the city's time as the center of the Dutch East India Company.

# The Melting Pot

Later, but still in ancient times, groups of short black folk (Negritos) and heavy-browed people, something like the aborigines of Australia today, moved into this area. Following them came taller brown-skinned peoples. You may see traces of all these human breeds in the large western islands. Out of Asia came still others, this time of a more "Mongoloid" or Malayan type. They gradually flooded the coastal areas, and in the western islands nearly submerged the older groups. In other areas they married and mixed to form intermediate peoples like the Alfurs of the Molucca region. Added to the melting pot during the last 2,000 years have been Hindus from India, Arabs, Chinese, and finally European peoples, all mingling to some extent.

As you go back from the coastal cities to the mountains, and as you pass from east to west through the Indies, you will be able to trace this story roughly in the many different peoples you see.

All this accounts for the development of so many different kinds of local custom and speech. For instance, there are today at least 250 major language groups in the area. You'll find, too, that the peoples of the Indies are still first and foremost citizens of their own ancestral localities.

*From the US Army Pocket Guide to Netherlands East Indies*

*Local musicians*

# Religions

Indonesia officially recognizes six religions: Islam, Protestantism, Catholicism, Hinduism, Buddhism, and Confucianism. However, it has been estimated that there may be over 200 non-official religions practiced in the country and many of those that practice one of the six official religions combine those beliefs with the spiritual or animist indigenous practices. The religious history of Indonesia is long and heavily influenced by immigration and trade with Europe, China, and India.

# An Absence of Bigotry

*Sir Thomas Raffles, the founder of Singapore, was also the governor of the East Indies during the brief period of British rule from the following excerpt on religion is from his work* The History of Java *published in 1817.*

The natives are still devotedly attached to their ancient institutions, and though they have long ceased to respect the temples and idols of a former worship, they still retain a high respect for the laws, usages, and national observances which prevailed before the introduction of Mahomedanism. And although some few individuals among them may aspire to a higher sanctity and closer conformity to Mahomedanism than others, it may be fairly stated, that the Javans in general, while they believe in one supreme God, and that Mahomed was his Prophet, and observe some of the outward forms of the worship and observances, are little acquainted with the doctrines of that religion, and are the least bigoted of its followers. Few of the chiefs decline the use of wine, and if the common people abstain from inebriating liquors, it is not from any religious motive. Mahomedan institutions, however, are still gaining ground, and with a free trade a great accession of Arab teachers might be expected to arrive. Property usually descends according to the Mahomedan law but in other cases, the Mahomedan code, as adopted by the Javans, is strangely blended with the more ancient institutions of the country.

*Bay at Batavia*

# The Bell That Links Batavia and China

*This is a story told by R.F. Johnston in his book* Buddhist China, *about a bell from a monastery on the island of Putuo, off the coast of eastern China, which was (and remains) an important center of Buddhism with many temples. It was said in the "Ta-Chih" monastery that the great bell was stolen by Europeans of an unknown nationality and conveyed to "their capital in the country of Europe" where it was hung in a gateway. One day, the bell fell down and sank in the soft ground and was forgotten. Then in 1723, the bell sounded and the local people dug it up in amazement. Chinese merchants acquired the bell and shipped it back to the monastery in 1733. Mr Johnston takes up the story from there.*

There is no reason to doubt that the story as thus told in the annals of the monastery is substantially true; but it seems improbable that the monks were correct in their belief that the bell had actually been conveyed to Europe. The Chinese of those days had very vague ideas of geography, and the monks of Pootoo had evidently no very distinct knowledge of the political divisions of the 'country of Europe.'

Perhaps the bell did not make quite so long a journey as they supposed. The suggestion may be hazarded that its resting place during the period from 1665 to 1723 was no European town, but Batavia, a city of the Dutch East Indies, and though its old ramparts no longer exist, it was a strong walled town in the seventeenth and eighteenth centuries. Possibly the Chinese story of the fall of the bell at the gates of the city, and its subsequent disappearance until its presence underground was revealed by a sound like rolling thunder, is based on the historical fact that in 1699 Batavia was visited by a destructive earthquake.

Thus the real course of events may have been something like this: the bell was carried from Pootoo to Java in 1655; it was suspended in a tower on the wall of the city of Batavia; it remained there till 1699, when the wall was destroyed by an earthquake; it lay buried under the ruins of the wall until 1723; and in that year, after it had disappeared from view for almost a quarter of a century, the removal of the debris restored it to the light of day, The inscription on the bell, we may suppose, was read by Chinese residents in Java, who learned thereby the name of the monastery to which it originally belonged. Through them the story may easily have come to the ears of the Chinese merchants of Fukien, who at that time controlled a large proportion of China's foreign trade.

# Hinduism and Buddhism

Hinduism was first introduced to the islands around the 2nd century, closely followed by Buddhism in the 4th century. The history of the two religions is closely tied as they both were established and quickly spread around the 5th century. In the 9th century, at the peak of Buddhist and Hindu influence on the islands, Prambanan, a Hindu temple, and Borobudur, the world's largest Buddhist temple, were built on the island of Java.

*An 1873 photo of Borobudur, the world's largest Buddhist temple built in the 9th century, with a Dutch flag flying from the top. The monument was rediscovered in 1814 by Sir Thomas Stamford Raffles, during a short period of British rule, after centuries of abandonment. Today the monument is a World Heritage Site and one of Indonesia's largest tourist attractions.*

*An 1859 illustration of ruins of Prambanan, a Hindu temple built in the 9th century, and rediscovered in 1811 during a short period of British rule under Sir Thomas Stamford Raffles. Today, the monument is a World Heritage Site.*

# Islam

Indonesia is home to the world's largest Muslim population, almost 90% of the country's population. First introduced to the islands in the 14th century, by the 15th century Islam had become the dominant religion of the region. Islam as practiced in Indonesia is generally viewed as being more tolerant and flexible than in some other regions of the world.

## Christianity: Protestantism and Catholicism

Though Catholicism and Protestantism are both Christian faiths, they are treated as separate religions by the government of Indonesia. Catholicism was first introduced to the East Indies in 1534 when the Portuguese arrived in the Islands. After the Dutch took over, Catholicism was banned and the Dutch state religion of Protestantism replaced it. Today, Protestants comprise the majority of Christians in Indonesia.

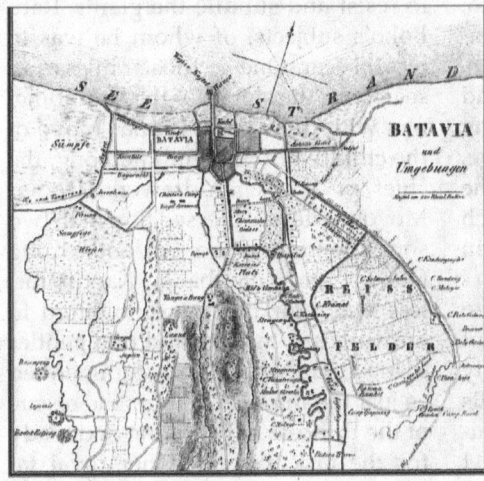

Batavia 1840

## Unifying Force

*From E.M. Beekman's introduction to P.A. Daum's Ups & Downs of Life in the Indies*

Religion was a major factor in the fortunes of Indonesia. The Portuguese expansion was in part a result of Portugal's crusade against Islam, which was quite as ferocious and intransigent as the holy war of the Mohammedans. Islam may be considered a unifying force in the archipelago; it cut across all levels of society and provided a rallying point for resistance to foreign intrusion. Just as the Malay language had done linguistically, Islam proved to be a syncretizing force when there was no united front. One of the causes of Portugal's demise was its inflexible antagonism to Islam, and later the Dutch found resistance to their rule fueled by religious fervor as well as political dissatisfaction.

# The Legend of the Giant King

*The legend tells the story of Prince Band-ung Bondowoso who has fallen in love with Princess Rara Jonggrang, daughter of Ratu Boku the giant king. The prince kills the king in battle and so he is rejected by the princess. Eventually, at the prince's insistence, she agrees to the marriage if he will build one thousand temples in one night.The prince calls forth spirits to help him with his task and, when the prince is about to complete the final temple, the princess tricks the spirits into believing that it is morning, causing them to flee. The prince is so angered by the trick that he curses Rara Jonggrang to stone, making her the last statue and completing his task. The image to the left is the final statue of the princess.*

*Temple of the PRAMBANAN GROUP in 1895*

*From* Monumental Java(), *by J.F. Scheltema*

Once upon a time Prambanan was ruled by a giant-king, Ratu Boko, possessed of an only daughter, Princess Jonggrang, and an adopted son, Raden Gupolo, whose father had been killed by command of the King of Pengging. Having sworn revenge, Raden Gupolo feigned love for the beautiful daughter of that monarch and asked Ratu Boko to assist him in making her his wife. Ambassadors were despatched with instructions to negotiate the marriage. His Majesty of Pengging received them in a friendly manner and entertained them at his Court but, not wanting Raden Gupolo for a son-in-law, he sent secret agents in all directions to seek and bind to his service a hero with power to resist and subdue the giants, Ratu Boko's subjects, of whom he was in mortal fear. One of those emissaries, searching the slopes of the Soombing, met with the recluse Damar Moyo of the children of Sumendi Petoong, the chief of the legèn-drawers. Damar Moyo's wife had blessed him with two sons, Bondowoso, a tall and strong fellow, and Bambang Kandilaras, less muscular but more favoured in outward appearance and of a gentler disposition, whom he recommended as just the man needed for the rescue of the Princess of Pengging and ready for the task, provided her royal father would consent, in consideration

of the defeat of the giants, to give his daughter to the young man with half his kingdom as dowry and the other half to follow after his death—which conditions prove that even in those remote days the saintly did not despise worldly advantage. The King of Pengging consented and Bambang Kandilaras marched against Prambanan, but no weapon could harm Ratu Boko, who roared so dreadfully that the sound and his breath combined were enough to knock any hu-

man foe down at a distance too far to distinguish a man from a woman or a giant from a waringin-tree. Bambang Kandilaras fled, reporting at Damar Moyo's cave, and was commanded to try once more with the assistance of his brother Bondowoso. They accomplished nothing. Bambang Kandilaras ran away even before the battle commenced, to hide himself in a ravine where the troops of Prambanan could

not follow him, and Bondowoso, blown off his legs by a puff from Ratu Boko's formidable lungs, sought safety in precipitate retreat to the mountain Soombing. Then Damar Moyo taught him a magical word which, pronounced twice, would make him big and heavy as an elephant, and give him the strength of a thousand of those animals. Thus armed, Bondowoso returned to Prambanan, where he killed half of Ratu Boko's warriors in their sleep, while the other half, waking up, concentrated backward, with the enemy in hot pursuit, to tell their king what had happened. Nobody shall stir, said he; I myself alone will settle this little business. Meeting Bondowoso near the village Tangkisan, he began to roar as loud and fume as hard as he could but, to his astonishment, his breath lacked the accustomed power and so he had to fight for his life hand to hand. It was a terrible fight: houses and gardens were trampled down, forests rooted up and mountains kicked over, while the perspiration dripping from the bodies of the enraged combatants formed a large pool, the Telaga Powiniyan. To end the struggle, Bondowoso, in a supreme effort, seized Ratu Boko round the middle and threw him into that pool, where he sank and, drowning, made the earth tremble with a last roar of anger and distress. Raden Gupolo, hearing the noise, hastened to his assistance with a few drops of the water of life in a cup, an elixir prepared by Mboq Loro Jonggrang, — only a few drops, but enough to resuscitate the dead giant-king if put to his lips. Bambang Kandilaras, however, drew

## Rara Jonggrang means Slender Virgin in Javanese

his bow and, from the place where he had watched the fight, shot the cup out of the hand of Raden Gupolo, who thereupon attacked Bondowoso. Bambang Kandilaras let more arrows fly at the giant-warriors of Prambanan, who now rushed up to avenge

their king's death. In the general mêlée Bondowoso killed also Raden Gupolo and cut off his head, which he threw away in an easterly direction, changing it into a mountain, the Gunoong Gampeng; but his brains and heart he threw away in a southwesterly direction, changing them into another mountain, the Gunoong Woongkal. Thereupon he defeated the remaining half of the army of Prambanan and repaired to Pengging, claiming the reward for his brother. The king of that country, glad to be rid of the giants, was as good as his word, wedded his beautiful daughter to Bambang Kandilaras and appointed Bondowoso his viceroy in Prambanan, with the rank and title of bupati. Taking up his abode in the palace of the late Raden Gupolo, Bondowoso happened to see Mboq

Loro Jonggrang, who continued living in the kraton of Ratu Boko, and fell in love with her. He asked her hand in marriage and she, abhorring the man who had killed her father, and one so unprepossessing in countenance too, but afraid to provoke his displeasure by a blank refusal, answered that she was willing to become his wife on condition of his providing a suitable sasrahan or wedding-present, nothing more nor less than six deep wells in six buildings, the like of which no mortal eye had ever seen, with a thousand statues of the former kings of Prambanan and their divine ancestors, the gods in heaven, all to be dug and built and carved in one night. Bondowoso called in the help of his father, the recluse Damar Moyo, of the King of Pengging and of his brother Bambang Kandilaras, all three of whom responded, going to Prambanan and uniting in prayer on the day before the night agreed upon by the spirits of the lower regions, who had been commandeered for the task by the saint of the mountain Soombing. The evening fell and as soon as darkness enveloped the earth a weird sound was heard of invisible hands busy laying foundations, erect-

*Prambanan Group today*

ing walls and sculpturing statuary. By half past three o'clock the six wells were dug, the six buildings completed and nine hundred and ninety-nine statues standing in their places. But Mboq Loro Jonggrang, roused from her slumbers by the hammering and chiselling, and suspecting what was going on, ordered her handmaidens out to stamp the padi and to strew the ground, where the noise was loudest, with flowers and to sprinkle perfume. The spirits of the lower regions cannot bear the odour of flowers and perfumes, as everybody knows; so they had to desist and deserted their almost finished work in precipitate flight, to the consternation of Bondowoso, who pronounced this curse: Since the girls of Prambanan take pleasure in fooling a faithful suitor, may the gods grant that they shall have to wait long before they become brides! Having said this, yet hoping against hope, he called on his lady, who asked tauntingly whether the honour of his visit meant the announcement that the task imposed upon him by way of testing his love, had been completed. This filled the measure and he answered: No, it is not and you shall complete it yourself. The threat was immediately realised: Loro Jonggrang changed into a statue of stone, the thousandth, which terminated the labour of the spirits and is still to be seen in a niche on the north side of the principal edifice independent their propensity to it is so great that it resembles rather a serious occupation than a sport. You seldom meet a man travelling in the country.

*A Javanese woman in 1897*

# Women's Clothing

*Clothing as described by Harry de Windt in* Across the Equator *published in 1882*

The morning costume of the European lady in Java is apt to take a stranger by surprise. It consists of the Malay "sarong," a loose clinging silk skirt which reaches to the ankles, the upper garment being the "Kabarga," a long embroidered white linen jacket. The hair is worn loose, and the bare feet are thrust into half slippers embroidered with real gold and silver beads. This dress is worn from early morning till five o'clock in the afternoon, the Batavia calling hour. This costume has one great advantage, that of coolness, and would doubtless look becoming on a pretty woman, though as that article is very seldom, if ever, seen in Java, we had no opportunity of judging.

# Eating at the Warong

*An excerpt from the book* Java Facts and Fancies *by Augusta De Wit, published in 1905*

"After the bath, the Javanese proceeds to take his morning meal; and this, again is a public performance. The noon repast—the only solid one in the day—is prepared and eaten at home. But, for the morning and evening meals, the open air and the cuisine of the warong are preferred. The warong is the native restaurant. There are many kinds and varieties of it: from its most simple and compendious shape—two wooden cases, the one containing food,

*A Batavian warong*

prepared and raw, the other, a chafing-dish full of live coals, and a supply of crockery—to its fully-developed form, the atap- covered hut. There, a dozen, and more customers hold their symposia presided over by the owner, who sits cross-legged on the counter amid heaps of fruit, vegetables, and confectionery. All manner of men meet here: drivers of sadoos or hack carriages, small merchants, artizans, Government clerks, policemen, water-carriers, servants, hadjis, not to mention the "corresponding" womankind. They talk, they talk! and they laugh! The affairs of all Batavia are discussed here—matters of business, intrigue, love, money, office, everything, material to make a Javanese Decamerone of, if a Boccaccio would but come and put it into shape. There are several of these warongs about Tanah-Abang and the Koningsplein, and, of course, in the native quarters. But the smaller, portable ones are found everywhere: by the river-side, at the railway stations, at the sadoo-stands, along the canals, at the corners of the streets; and they seem to do a thriving business."

73

# The World's First Multinational Corporation

The Dutch East India Company, known as Vereenigde Oostindische Compagnie or VOC in Dutch, was officially formed in 1602 under sponsorship of the Dutch government to create a monopoly over the spice trade. This agreement was to only last 21 years, instead it lasted for 200.

After its formation, the VOC set up its first trading post in Banten on the western coast of Java, another at Jayakarta – later Batavia – with the Company's headquarters in Ambon. Then, in 1619, the Company took Batavia from the local population in a violent conquest and reestablished its headquarters there, a more convenient location for trade and far enough away from the British and Portuguese competition. The VOC began to expand its interests beyond Java, further colonizing the Indonesian archipelago, Ceylon – now known as Sri Lanka – and the Cape of Good Hope in Africa. By 1669, the Dutch East India Company was the richest company in the world with a monopoly on the spice trade, and in possession of 40 warships, 150 trading vessels, and 10,000 professional soldiers on top of the many employees and subjects as well as semi-governmental powers such as declaring war, prosecuting criminals, negotiating treaties, and establishing colonies. The VOC was also the first ever to issue stock and, between 1602 and 1696, paid out a regular dividend that yielded between 12% and 63%.

The Dutch East India Company controlled the trade in the East Indies and as the Company's headquarters, the city of Batavia grew in size and importance.

Yet, despite its early success and domination in the East Indies, the Company began to decline by the end of the 17th century and into the 18th. Wars in Europe disrupted trade and, along with loss of trade with Japan and China and the growth of other European trading companies, the Dutch East India Company could no longer keep up. In 1800, the Company was formally dissolved and all of its colonial possessions were brought under the control of the Dutch government.

*A drawing of Sir Lancaster's ship, the Red Dragon, which he sailed on the East India Company's first voyage*

# Dutch East India Company
## (Vereenigde Oostindische Compagnie, VOC)

*The logo of the Dutch East India company comes uses the letters VOC from its Dutch name Vereenigde Oostindische Compagnie. The logo was in use throughout the company's tenure and was on various items, from cannons to coins. The logo also appeared on the company's flag and uniforms. An additional letter was sometimes used atop the standard logo to designate which chamber or branch was conducting the operation (such as the logo of the Amsterdam chamber shown here).*

# A Colonial Friendship

*From* Monumental Java *by J.F. Scheltema, M.A., 1912*

When the East India Company began to make its influence felt, Moslim solidarity proved a valuable asset as, for instance, in the relations with Bantam and Cheribon, whose Pangeran proposed the title of Susuhunan for Ageng (1625) before Mecca promoted him to the Sooltanate (1630). In 1628 and 1629 he ventured to attack Batavia, the new settlement of the Dutch, but had to retire and, what was even worse, by provoking those upstart strangers, he damaged his trade: they closed the channels of export to Malacca and other foreign ports of rice, the principal produce of the land. "Mataram must now become our friend," wrote the Governor-General to his masters, the Honourable Seventeen, and, indeed, Mangku Rat I., Ageng's son, found himself obliged to sign a treaty of friendship with the Company—a dangerous friendship! Differences between their "friend" and Bantam with Cheribon were sedulously fostered by the authorities at Batavia; the Company took a hand in the putting down of disturbances created in East Java by Taruna Jaya of Madura and Kraëng Galesoong of Macassar; the Company patronised and protected the reigning Sooltans, who moved their residence from Karta to Kartasura, against pretenders and exacted payment in land, privileges, concessions, monopolies, etc., shamelessly in excess of the real or pretended assistance afforded in quelling purposely manufactured anarchy—precisely as we see it happen nowadays wherever western civilisation offers her "disinterested" services to eastern countries of promising complexion for exploitation by western greed.

*A beer hall in Soerabaja, early 20th century*

*"Netherland's Most Precious Jewel"*

# The Company's Colonization

*From* Monumental Java *by J.F. Scheltema, M.A., 1912*

The foundation of Batavia on the site of old Yacatra, taken by Jan Pietersz Coen, May 30, 1619, had meant, among other things, an always keener competition in trade with Bantam or, rather, the "establishment of a free rendezvous", i.e. free of bickerings with native princes and princelings, for the fleets of the Company on their long voyage to the Moluccos. Bantam having outstripped Cheribon by the importance she derived from English and Dutch shipping, resented the blow which threatened to relegate her to a second or third place, and this resulted in frequent conflicts with the intruders, though the boundary line of their settlement and their mutual relationship had been carefully de-

fined in the treaty of 1659. On the other side in occasional difficulties with Mataram, the Company, acting on the divide et impera principle, encouraged the rivalry between the middle and western empires, which both strove for supremacy in the Priangan. How the Company accomplished its purpose and triumphed, needs here no detailed examination. Its objects and the considerations which moved it, are wittily discussed in a Javanese mock-epic, the Serat Baron Sakendher, a satire on the rise of Dutch power at Batavia, the foundation of Moor Yang Koong (Jan Pietersz Coen). If that pattern of regents outre mer, the first Dutch Governor-General in Java, whose motto was

*Dutch arrival in Jacarta (renamed Batavia) in 1618*

"never despair", whose grip like the grip of the tiger, has invited comparison with Ganesa (firstborn of Siva and Parvati) for wisdom and cautious statecraft, with Skanda (also sprung from the Mahadeva's loins but without the Devi's collaboration) for resolution and mettle, here we find him as the son of Baron Sookmool, Baron Sakendher's brother, and Tanaruga, daughter of the Pajajaranese Princess Retna Sakar Mandhapa, and the poet makes the personification of the Company say to his twelve hopefuls, the earliest Tuan Tuan Edeleer, or honourable members of the Governor-General's Council: Good measures you will enforce, without quarrelling amongst yourselves, and, even if it were larceny, the moment you have decided upon it by common consent, I give my permission, — a speech delightfully in keeping with the tactics of his father, whose artillery prevailed, not with iron cannon-balls, but with golden grapeshot of ducats and doubloons.

*Dutch arrival in Jacarta (renamed Batavia) in 1618*

# J.P. Coen and the Massacre of 1621

Jan Pieterszoon Coen was one of the most influential figures of the Dutch East India Company in shaping the region. Born in 1587, Coen grew into a man known for his willingness to use violence, strict beliefs, and mercilessness to those that opposed him. In one story, when a girl whom Coen had been entrusted to care for was found in the garden in the arms of a soldier, Coen had the soldier beheaded and the girl was only spared death by drowning, instead receiving a whipping, because she was underage. In 1617, Coen was appointed to his first term as governor-general of the East Indies by the Dutch East India Company. As governor-general, he began to direct more of the company's trade through what would be called Batavia, rather than Bantam, an English trading port on the island of Java, where they faced disputes with the locals, the Chinese, and the English. In 1619, after seizing control of Batavia from the local ruler by burning the city to the ground, Coen built a fort on the ruins and claimed the port for the Dutch.

One of the most violent acts committed by Coen was the massacre of the Bandanese on the Island of Bandaneira in 1621. The Dutch had created a monopoly in the trade of nutmeg through a treaty with the native populations prohibiting them from trading with anyone but the Dutch while paying the natives very little. To reinforce this monopoly, in 1621, Coen ordered the beheading of forty local leaders under perceived violations of the treaty. Coen and his men proceeded to massacre the rest of the local population, decimating their numbers from around 13,000-15,000 to only about 1,000. The remaining population was forced to work as slave labor in the nutmeg groves, along with people from Java and other islands brought in to replace the workforce.

*J.P. Coen, the founder of Batavia and Governor of the Dutch East Indies from 1617-1623*

# Trade in Batavia

*An excerpt from* Trade and Travel *in the Far East by G.F. Davidson, published in 1846*

What a joyous place was Batavia in those days, with every body thriving, and the whole town alive and bustling with an active set of merchants from all parts of the world! The Dutch Government, at that time, pursued a more liberal system than they have of late adopted; and, instead of monopolizing the produce of the Island, sold it by public auction regularly every month. This plan naturally attracted purchasers from England, the Continent of Europe, and the United States of America, who brought with them good Spanish dollars to pay for what they purchased; so that silver money was as plentiful in Netherlands India, in those days, as copper doits have since become. The enlightened individual who now governs Java and its dependencies, is, I have good reason to think, opposed to the monopolizing system pursued by his Government: his hands, however, are tied, and he can only remonstrate, while the merchants can but pray that his remonstrances may be duly weighed by his superiors. Java exports one million peculs of coffee per annum, one million peculs of rice, and one million peculs of sugar; besides vast quantities of tin, pepper, hides, indigo, &c.

*An advertisement for the Royal Packet Navigation Company, a Dutch shipping company that operated from 1888 to 1966 in the Dutch East Indies. The company supported the economic connections between the islands in the Dutch East Indies and worked hard to ensure that all inter-island trade went through Batavia, rather than the British port of Singapore.*

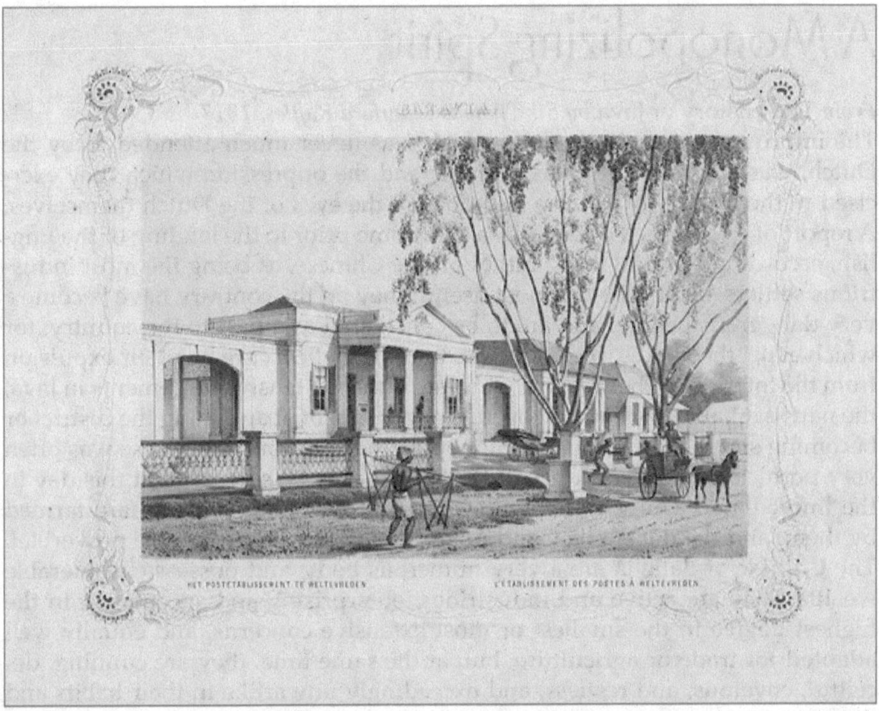
HET POSTETABLISSEMENT TE WELTEVREDEN
L'ETABLISSEMENT DES POSTES A WELTEVREDEN

BRIEFKAART
uit Nederlandsch-Indië.
'sGravenhage
(Holland)

Groet
van Sumatra's
Westkust.

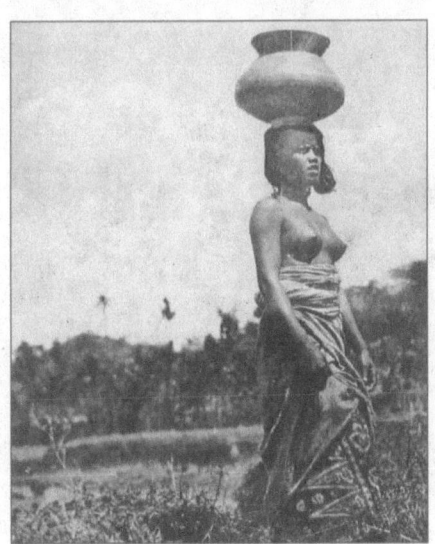

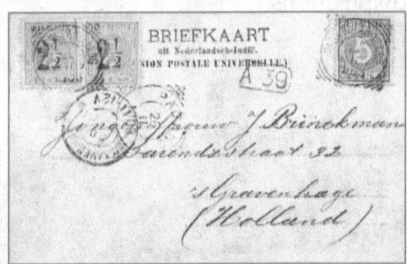

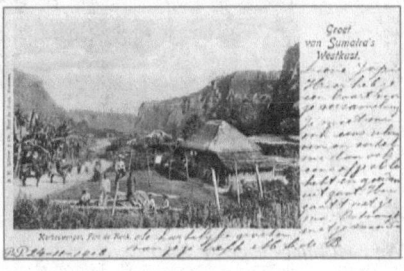

# A Monopolizing Spirit

*From* The History of Java *by Sir Thomas Stamford Raffles, 1817*
The improvement of the people, which was never much attended to by the
Dutch, was still less so by the Chinese, and the oppression which they exer-
cised in the vicinity of Batavia had opened the eyes of the Dutch themselves.
A report of the Council of Batavia, a short time prior to the landing of the English, accordingly states, that " although the Chinese, as being the most industrious settlers, should be the most useful, they on the contrary have become a
very dangerous people, and are to be considered as a pest to the country; for
which evil," they add, " there appears to be no radical cure but their expulsion
from the interior." Wherever the Chinese formed extensive settlements in Java,
the native inhabitants had no alternative but that of abandoning the district or
becoming slaves of the soil. The monopolizing spirit of the Chinese was often
very pernicious to the produce of the soil, as may be seen even at this day in
the immediate vicinity of Batavia, where all the public markets are farmed
by them, and the degeneracy and poverty of the lower orders are proverbial.
The Chinese of Batavia are a very numerous body, and possess considerable
wealth. They are active and industrious, enterprising and speculative in the
highest degree in the smallest or most extensive concerns, and equally well
adapted for trade or agriculture; but, at the same time, they are cunning, de-
ceitful, covetous, and restless, and exceedingly unwarlike in their habits and
dispositions.

*An East Indies house, c.1920*

*A celebration in Batavia*

# Geger Pacinan, or the Chinatown Tumult

It had been the practice of many of the earliest governors of the Dutch East Indies to encourage Chinese immigration, employing them as skilled artisans, traders, shopkeepers, and workers in the sugar mills. Trade between China and the East Indies grew rapidly and by 1740 the Chinese population in Batavia had grown to well over 2,500 households. With the rise in population and the relative economic success of the Chinese as compared to the locals, the population was regarded with heavy suspicion and resentment from both the native population and the Dutch.

Following a devastating malaria outbreak during the 1730s, the Dutch instituted a new policy of deportation of Chinese who failed to carry proper identification cards, creating mistrust and unrest among the Chinese and leading many to desert their jobs. In 1740 large numbers of Chinese had gathered outside of Batavia, coming in from nearby settlements, and the Dutch governor issued an order that any uprising was to be dealt with using deadly force. On October 7, rumors had spread that the Chinese – who had begun arming themselves following the governor's announce-

*A drawing of the 1740 Batavia Massacre, dating from around 1895*

ment – were plotting against other ethnic groups in Batavia, leading to a large scale burning of Chinese houses and Chinese owned establishments while Dutch troops fired cannons into the homes in the Chinese district of the city. The Dutch then established a reward of two ducats for every Chinese head, sufficiently dealing with the survivors of the initial assault and engaging the other ethnic groups of the city. Eventually, on October 22, the governor called an end to the killings though violence and skirmishes continued. It is believed that at least 10,000 Chinese were killed within two weeks, with the number of survivors ranging anywhere from 600 to 3,000. The violence and distrust left behind by the massacre led to the Java War from 1741 to 1743, between Chinese/Javanese forces and the eventually victorious Dutch forces.

*Van Imhoff and two fellow councilmen were arrested for insubordination after going against Valckenier.*

*Adriaan Valckenier (1695-1751). While serving as Governor-General, he ordered the killing of many ethnic Chinese residents*

*Van Imhoff was sent to the Netherlands, but later assigned as the new governor-general of the Dutch East Indies.*

# The Moluccas

The Molucca Islands are the chain of islands in eastern Indonesia most often-referred to as the Spice Islands. Banda Island, one of the islands in the chain, was the only producer of nutmeg during early colonial times. This made the islands very important to European trade and economic interests. The first Europeans to visit the island chain were the Portuguese in the early 1500s, and for a while they were able to successfully control the spice trade to Europe. However, the Dutch and the English were not to be left out and the islands became a major conflict zone until the Dutch took complete control of the islands. To gain control of the last island, Run Island, they agreed to do a trade with England, handing over the island of Manhattan in North America in return. the relative value of the two islands has changed somewhat in the years since the agreement was executed.

*A Portuguese fort on the island of Ternate, one of the islands in the Moluccas in eastern Indonesia*

# THE DUTCH EAST INDIES.

## FROM SINGAPORE TO BATAVIA.

### HIGH TARIFFS AND LARGE CROWDS—THE MAIL SERVICE IN THE EAST—SAMPLES OF " DUTCH STUPIDITY "—SHREWDNESS OF COLONIAL MANAGEMENT—RESOURCES OF JAVA—TRADE OF BATAVIA—AMERICAN GOODS FOR THE JAVANESE MARKET— THE STREET RAILWAY QUESTION.

*From a Special Correspondent.*

Batavia, Java, Saturday,
Dec. 1, 1877.

The voyage from Singapore to Batavia is an affair of 40 or 50 hours, with a distance of 550 miles. The course is not the safest in the world, as there are numerous islands in the way, many shoals, and an inconveniently large number of currents. Possibly the dangers of the navigation may be the reason for the enormously high passage-$46 in coin, or very nearly $1 an hour. As if this were not enough, they crowd the steamers to excess, and are not over particular about white lies and that sort of thing to obtain them...

The steamer that brings you here anchors in the open roadstead forming the harbor, and you have a long journey to land. You have a mile of open water, and sometimes two miles of it, and then you have two miles of canal where the boatmen land and tow the craft by means of a long line. You meet boats like your own, and you meet small steamers on their way to the shipping... You seek a carriage and drive away to the hotel you have selected, and are somewhat surprised to find that the hotels are not in the town of Batavia, but at least two miles beyond it. You are inclined to set it down as a piece of Dutch stupidity in locating the hotels so far from the business centre, but when you come to pay for your carriage you find that Dutch stupidity has reached its zenith...

But somehow, in spite of their apparent obstuseness, they have managed their affairs on this island with wonderful shrewdness, and evinced a thorough knowledge of the process of running a colony. Java and the dependent islands are a source of great wealth to the Dutch Government, and no part of the energies of the people or the capabilities of the country are allowed to run to waste....

No part of Batavia is visible from the sea; the coast is low and flat, and there is little also beyond a forest of palm and other trees to greet the eye of the stranger. The town itself is not of great extent, but the suburbs and environs are something enormous, and make a city of magnificent distances. The houses are rarely more than of one story, and each has a surrounding of garden and tropical trees, so that a great deal of shade and recreation ground is secured. A canal with several branches runs through all of this area, and serves a

triple purpose. Boats may navigate it, people may wash their own bodies or the clothes of other people in it, and servants may empty all sorts of sewage material into it...

The chief business of Batavia is one of export; the imports are not heavy, as the country produces the most that the natives want, and the foreign population is not very large. European cloths, shoes, and wines are the heaviest imports, and they are chiefly for the consumption of the Dutch and other foreign residents. America has but little trade here save in what she buys; she sells occasional lots of carriages, chairs, hardware, ice, and petroleu,. The latter article is the most important of all and sometimes commands a high price; so much is this the case that the native merchants buy up the empty cans and fill them with a mixture of petroleum and some vegetable-oil that burns poorly, and gives a most wretched light...

# Staging Post

*From the US Army Pocket Guide to Netherlands East Indies*
The Indies area is like a huge melting pot where, for thousands of years, different streams of humans have merged, and in turn, spilled over eastward into the farther islands of the Pacific.

*Street in Batavia.*

# Destruction for Profit

*From* The History of Java *by Sir Thomas Stamford Raffles, 1817*

If the nutmeg and clove trees were allowed to grow where Providence would seem to have ordained that in their natural course they should, and this trade were opened to a free commerce, nutmegs might perhaps be procured as cheap as betel-nut, and cloves as cheap as pepper. "In the Spice Islands," observes Adam Smith, "the Dutch are said to burn all the spiceries which a fertile season produces beyond what they expect to dispose of in Europe, with such a profit as they think sufficient. In the islands where they have no settle-

ments they give a premium to those who collect the blossoms and green leaves of the clove and nutmeg trees which naturally grow there, but which this savage policy has now, it is said, completely exterminated. Even in the islands where they have settlements, they have very much reduced, it is said, the number of those trees. If the produce even of their own islands was much greater than what suited their market, the natives, they suspect, might find means to convey some part of it to other nations; and the best way, they imagine, to secure

Zandvoort
Tandjong-Priok-Java
38-B

their own monopoly, is to take care that no more shall grow than what they themselves carry to market. By different acts of oppression, they have reduced the population of the Moluccas nearly to the number which is sufficient to supply with fresh provisions and other necessaries of life, their own insignificant garrisons, and such of their ships as occasionally come there for a cargo of spices. Under the government of the Portuguese, however, these islands are said to have been tolerably well peopled."

From authentic accounts it appears, that they attempted to destroy and eradicate from a vast range of countries the most advantageous produce of the land, in order to favour their own petty traffic, and burnt a large proportion of the residue, in order to keep up their monopoly price in Europe on a small proportion of this produce.

# Nutmeg and Run Island

Nutmeg, until the middle of the 19th century, was only found on Run Island in the Banda Islands chain, part of the Molucca or Spice Islands in the East Indies. Highly prized and very expensive, in Europe, the spice was even thought to ward off the Plague. The Portuguese were the first of the Europeans to arrive at the Banda Islands around 1512 and, although they were unable to set up a permanent trading post, they brought back enough nutmeg and other spices to break through the Arabic monopoly in the spice trade. The Portuguese maintained control of the trade until the 17th century when the English and the Dutch entered the region and began a war for domination of the region. The Dutch were eventually victorious in 1667 after trading the island of Manhattan to the English for Run Island and began to build a monopoly on the nutmeg trade through the Dutch East India Company, often using violent methods. To keep nutmeg prices high, they burned fields of the trees that produce the nutmeg and would even burn their warehouses in the Netherlands to reduce the available supply. In 1760, it cost between 85 and 90 schilling to buy a pound of nutmeg in London, between £544.04 and £576.04 in today's prices. The profits for the Dutch were high, the spice selling at a price 300 times greater than what it cost to produce. The Dutch monopoly lasted for 200 years until the early 1800s when the British briefly gained control of the island and began to move trees to Singapore, Granada in the Caribbean and Zanzibar in Africa.

# Slavery in Batavia

*From* The History of Java *by Sir Thomas Stamford Raffles, 1817*

The native Javans are never reduced to this condition; or if they should happen to be seized and sold by pirates, a satisfactory proof of their origin would be sufficient to procure their enfranchisement. The slave merchants have therefore been under the necessity of resorting to the neighbouring islands for a supply, and the greatest number have been procured from Bdli and Celebes. The total amount may be estimated at about thirty thousand.

# Magical Hair

*From* Java Facts and Fancies *by Augusta De Wit, 1905*

"In Javanese fairy tales the long locks of nymphs and goddesses are treasured as talismans by the hero who has been fortunate enough to obtain one. There is great virtue for instance, in the long hair of the Pontianak, the cruel sprite that haunts the waringin tree. Have you never seen her glide by, white in the silver moonlight? Have you never heard her laugh, loud and long, when all was still? She is the soul of a dead virgin, whom no lover ever kissed. And now she cannot rest, because she never knew love; and she would fain win it yet; though not in kindness now, but in spite and deadly malice. She sits in the branches of trees, softly singing to herself as she combs her long hair. And when a young man, hearing her song, pauses to listen, she meets him, in the semblance of a maid fairer than the bride of the Love-god, and raises soft eyes to

him and smiling lips. But, when he would embrace her, he feels the gaping wound in her back, which she had concealed under her long hair. And, as he stands speechless with horror, she breaks away from him with a long loud laugh, and cries: "Thou hast kissed the Ponti-anak, thou must die!" And, ere the moon is full again, his kinsmen will have brought flowers to his grave. But, if he be quick-witted and courageous, he will seize the evil spirit by her flying locks; and, if he succeeds but in plucking out one single hair, he will not die, but live to a great age, rich, honoured, and happy, the husband of a Rajah's daughter and the father of Princes."

*Oil painting of an Upper Class Dutch family in Batavia in the 18th century*

# Mutiny on the Bounty

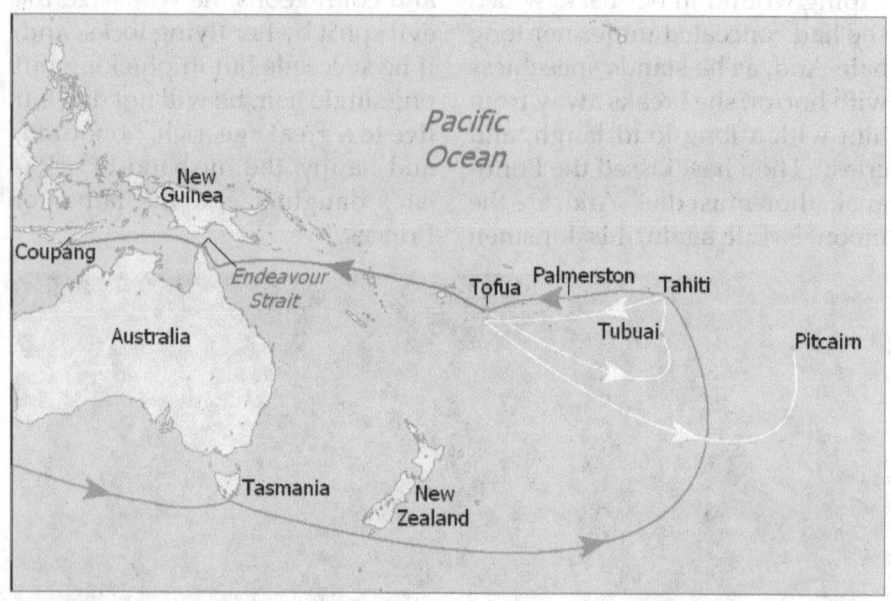

*Map showing the journey of Captain Bligh and the mutineers*

*Captain William Bligh of the HMS Bounty*

*An image of the breadfruit plant, a high-yielding fruit whose cooked flesh is often eaten in place of bread*

*Marlon Brando (left) as Fletcher Christian and Trevor Howard (middle) as Captain Bligh in the 1962 hit international film* Mutiny on the Bounty

The story of Captain Bligh and his mutinous crewmen have so captured the imagination as to inspire a novel and three different movies. In 1787, William Bligh set out from England with 44 men on the HMS Bounty on a mission to retrieve breadfruit plants from Tahiti and bring them to the West Indies to use as a source of food for the slaves on the plantations. During their time on the island of Tahiti the sailors became so enchanted by the island life that when they were set to sail with their cargo in 1789 they were led into a mutiny by Fletcher Christian, the Master's Mate, setting Captain Bligh and 18 loyal sailors adrift. Captain Bligh and his loyal men made their way with only a quadrant navigation device and a compass. The group made it through starvation, dehydration, and being chased by cannibals in Fiji to reach Timor and, finally Batavia, where they managed to secure passage home. Throughout their perilous journey, only five men were lost along the way. As for the mutineers, some stayed in Tahiti. These mutineers were eventually caught by the British Navy and held on the HMS Pandora, though this ship would eventually sink losing 4 prisoners and 31 crew members. The other mutineers set forth on the Bounty, including Christian Fletcher nine sailors, six Tahitian men, eighteen women, and one baby, to create a new settlement on the forgotten Pitcairn Island. This settlement, despite its bright prospects, failed as tensions rose until all but two of the Englishmen were killed by the Tahitians. Nevertheless, today, many of Pitcairn Island's residents are descendants of the mutineers and the Tahitians.

# A Kabaya and Trousers

*Augusta de Wit on the fashion of the Dutch East Indies, 1905*

A kabaya is a sort of dressing-jacket of profusely-embroidered white batiste, fastened down the front with ornamental pins and little gold chains; and under it is worn the sarong, a gaudily-coloured skirt falling down straight and narrow, with one single deep fold in front, and kept in place by a silk scarf wound several times round the waist, its ends dangling loose. With this costume, little high-heeled slippers are worn on the bare feet; and the hair is done in native style, simply drawn back from the forehead, and twisted into a knot at the back of the head. Altogether, this style of attire is original rather than becoming.

And, if this must be confessed of the ladies' costume, what must be said of the garb some men have the courage to appear in? A kabaya, and—may Mrs. Grundy graciously forgive me for saying it! for how shall I describe the indescribable, save by calling it by its own by me never-to-be-pronounced name?— A kabaya and trousers of thin sarong-stuff gaily sprinkled with blue and yellow flowers, butterflies, and dragons!

*Javanese dancing girls*

*A local restaurant, c. 1905*

*Depiction of a warong*

# Theater of the Wayang

*Depiction of a wayang*

*From* Java Facts and Fancies *by Augusta De Wit, 1905*

To all other pleasures, the Javanese prefers that of witnessing a performance of the wayang, the native theatre. He is an artist at heart, loving sweet sounds, graceful movements, and harmonies of bright colour; and all these he may enjoy at the wayang, where, in the pauses of the drama, ballads are sung to the tinkling accompaniment of the "gamellan," and splendidly-arrayed dancers put forth "the charm of woven paces and of waving hands." There are several kinds of "wayang," each having its own range of subjects and style of acting; the most ancient as well as the most popular, however, is the "wayang poerwa," the miniature stage on which the lives and adventures of Hindoo heroes, queens, and saints are acted over again by puppets of gilt and painted leather, moving in the hands of the "dalang," who recites the drama.

The "wayang poerwa" is best described as a combination of a "Punch-and-Judy" show and a kind of "Chinese shadows"; and — as with the famed shield which was silver on one side and gold on the other — its appearance depends upon the stand-point of the spectator. A puppet show to those in front of the screen, where the gaudily-painted figures are fixed in a piece of banana stem, it is a Chinese lantern to those on the other side, who see the shadows projected on the luminous canvas. According to ancient custom, the men sit in front and see the puppets; the women have their place behind the screen, and look on at the play of the shadows. In fully-equipped wayangs, as many as two hundred of these puppets are found, each with its own particular type and garb, characteristic of the person represented."

*Actors in the wayang*

# Krakatoa Awakened

*From* Blown to Bits or The Lonely Man of Rakata *by R.M. Ballantyne*

Krakatoa — destined so soon to play a thrilling part in the world's history; to change the aspect of the heavens everywhere; to attract the wondering gaze of nearly all nations, and to devastate its immediate neighbourhood — is of volcanic origin, and, at the time we write of (1883) was beginning to awaken from a long, deep slumber of two hundred years. Its last explosion occurred in the year 1680. Since that date it had remained quiet. But now the tremendous subterranean forces which had originally called it into being were beginning to reassert their existence and their power. Vulcan was rousing himself again and beginning once more to blow his bellows. So said some of the sailors who were constantly going close past the island and through Sunda Straits, which may be styled the narrows of the world's highway to the China seas.

## REUTER'S AGENCY.

**TERRIFIC ERUPTION.**

Batavia, August 27

A terrific eruption of Mount Krakatoa, in the Straits of Sunda, is taking place. The spectacle is a terribly grand one, and is visible nightly from Batavia. There has also been a disastrous irruption of the sea at Anjer and Serang, seaports of Java, and great damage has been done to both towns.

# THE ERUPTION OF KRAKATOA.

## DISAPPEARANCE OF TOWNS.

## SUNDA STRAITS MUCH CHANGED.

## GREAT LOSS OF LIFE AMONG EUROPEANS AND NATIVES.

[REUTER'S TELEGRAMS.]

Batavia, August 28, Noon.
All quiet. Sky clear. Communication with Serang restored. Telegraph inspector report, whilst trying to repair the line at Anjer early on the morning of the 27th saw high colum of sea approaching with roaring noise and fled inland. Knows nothing further of the fate of Anjer, but believes all lost

August 29, 10 A.M.
Sky continues clear. The temperature fell 10 degrees on the 27th. Now normal. Native huts all along the beach are washed away. Birds roosted during the ash rain, and cocks crowed as it cleared away. Fish dizzy. Town covered with thin layer of ashes giving the roads a quaint bright look. Sad news just coming from the west coast. Shall wire again.

11 A.M.
Anjer, Tjeringen, and Telokbetong destroyed.

11.20 A.M.
Eight houses at Sunda Straits have disappeared.

Noon.
Where once Mount Kramatau stood the sea now plays.

12.30 P.M.
Aspect at Sunda Straits much changed. Navigation dangerous.

1.50 P.M.
Intelligence from official sources announces that Anjer was completely destroyed by the tidal wave which followed the eruption of Krakatoa.

There was a great loss of life. The Merak quarries completely disappeared, all who were on the spot perishing except Nienwenhuis (?).

There has been enormous loss of life among both Europeans and natives in North Bantam. Property has also been damaged to an immense extent.

The floating dock at Onrust is adrift, severely damaged.

The war steamer Siak and the floating dock Amsterdam have been driven ashore at Purmerend. The Nederland Company's steamship Wilhelmina is also ashore at Priok.

Lloyd's agent at Batavia telegraphs under today's date as follows: "Volcanic eruption at Krakatoa, 27th of August. Great damage caused through tidal wave. Anjer completely destroyed. Navigation through Sunda probably changed."

Sunda Straits, through which passes a large portion of the trade of China, as also most of the trade of Batavia, Singapore, and other ports in the Java and China seas, separates the large islands of Java and Sumatra. Princes Channel and the Great Channel, both on the south side of the Straits, are the channels most commonly used. Krakatoa Island, the site of the eruption, bounds the Great Channel on the north side. Anjer, which was a large place on the north coast of Java, 78 miles from Batavia, was much frequented by vessels in want of supplies.

# THE ILLUSTRATED
# LONDON NEWS.

No. 2316.—VOL. LXXXIII.    SATURDAY, SEPTEMBER 8, 1883.    WITH TWO SUPPLEMENTS    SIXPENCE BY POST, 6½d.

ISLAND OF KRAKATOA, IN THE STRAITS OF SUNDA, THE CENTRE OF THE LATE VOLCANIC ERUPTION, SAID TO HAVE DISAPPEARED.

EAST COAST AND ISLANDS OF THE STRAITS OF SUNDA, WITH ANJER, A PORT OF JAVA.

THE STRAITS OF SUNDA, AS SEEN AFTER LEAVING ANJER.

THE VOLCANIC ERUPTION IN THE STRAITS OF SUNDA.

# Islands of Fire

Indonesia lies on the Ring of Fire, the zone in the Pacific home to over 75 percent of the world's volcanoes. Within the country itself, there are 150 volcanoes of which a little over 120 are still active today. Among the most active volcanoes are Kelud and Merapi on the island of Java with the latter erupting more than 80 times since the year 1000. Yet, Indonesia's most famous eruptions may be those of Mount Krakatoa in 1883 and the most devastating eruption of Mount Tambora in 1815. Mount Krakatoa, on the island of Krakatau to the north of Java, not only produced a massive eruption, but also a series of deadly tsunamis. The official death toll was given as a little over 36,000, most from the tsunamis. The most visible effect was the almost complete destruction of the island of Krakatau, now a third of its original size.

Yet, despite the damage wrought by Krakatoa, it was not the worst to be seen by the Dutch East Indies. Mount Tambora, on the island of Sumbawa to the south of Java, holds the record for the most powerful volcanic eruption in recorded history. The death count is estimated from 71,000 to 88,000 and the entire town of Tambora was wiped off the map. However, this volcano also managed to affect the entire globe, creating a global volcanic winter in 1816 that created a famine throughout Europe and the Americas. This worldwide phenomenon is known as The Year Without a Summer.

Mojo

Flores Sea

Mt. Tambora

Sanggar
Peninsula

*Volcanic activity at Anak Krakatau, 2008*

# Wave of Sound and Sea

*From* The Wonder Book of Volcanoes and Earthquakes *by Professor Edwin J. Houston, Ph.D., published in 1907*

That memorable Sunday of August 26th, 1883, came during a season of the year known as the dry monsoon, a name given the season of the periodical winds from the Indian Ocean. Batavia, and the surrounding country, greatly needed rain, for in this part of the world it seldom rains from April to October, although the air is very moist and damp. For this reason the beginning of the wet season is always welcomed. When, therefore, the rumbling sounds of the approaching catastrophe of Krakatoa were heard in Batavia, the people, believing that the noises were due to peals of thunder, rejoiced, for all thought they heralded an earlier setting in of the wet monsoon. But when the rumbling sounds increased and reports were heard like heavy artillery, it was clear that the sounds were the beginning of a volcanic eruption, a phenomenon with which they were only too well acquainted, but, as volcanic eruptions were far from being uncommon in Java, no one was very greatly frightened.

Besides the sound waves in the air, there were waves in the waters of the ocean. Suddenly, without any warning, the people of Batavia were surprised by a huge wave that, crossing the Straits of Sunda, entered the ship canal before referred to as connecting the city with the ocean, and, rising above the brick wall, poured over the surrounding country.

Although Batavia was 100 English miles from Krakatoa, yet after travelling this distance the wave was sufficiently strong to enter the city and flood its streets with water to a depth of several feet. Fortunately, the loss of life was small in the city of Batavia, but very great in the surrounding towns and villages.

The ocean waves varied in height at different times of the eruption. The greatest were from fifty to eighty feet high. Just imagine the effect of a wave twice the height of an ordinary house. The waves caused great damage to the shipping in the neighborhood. In one instance, a vessel was carried one and a half miles inland and left on dry land thirty feet above the level of the sea.

# DE L'ASIE. 143

## FIGURE LXII.

# Floods Floods Floods

The city of Batavia and Jakarta have been subject to flooding right from the start of the settlement, suggesting the location choice was not ideal. The first serious flooding to be recorded occurred in 1621, just a few years after the Dutch first landed, but that incident was followed by similar inundations in many other years. We present here a few images from some of those many floods.

## Floods 1922

## Floods 1925

## Floods 1932

# Headhunting

The Dayaks are the native people of Borneo, the term used to loosely describe the many different smaller groups with their own customs, languages, laws, and culture. One practice that is common across Dayaks groups is headhunting: the practice of taking and preserving a person's head after killing them. The practice of headhunting can be found around the world and is done for varying reasons. Some reasons for the Dayaks headhunting are to add supernatural strength of the soul believed to be found in the head, revenge, a dowry for marriages, for a better harvest or to reinforce buildings, and to display social status and power. Headhunting was largely abandoned by the early 1900s from the spread of Christianity as old religions were abandoned and bans by the colonial powers, though there was a brief resurgence during World War II when the allied powers encouraged headhunting against the Japanese.

*A Dayak chief in full war dress, a photograph from the 19th century*

# Raden Saleh

Raden Saleh Sjarif Boestaman was a Indonesia artist born in 1811 who developed a highly individual style combining European painting techniques with local styles and subjects. He is sometimes described as an Indonesian Romantic painter and the pioneer of modern Indonesian art. He died in 1880 at the age of 68.

*Raden Saleh c. 1840*

*Raden Saleh painting of the arrest of Pangeran Diponegoro in 1857, c. 1857-1880*

117

# The Pursuit of Staying Cool

*From* Java Facts and Fancies *by Augusta De Wit, 1905*

For to be cool, or not to be cool, that is the great question, and all things are arranged with a view to solving it in the most satisfactory manner possible. For the sake of coolness, one has marble floors or Javanese matting instead of carpets, cane-bottomed chairs and settees in lieu of velvet-covered furniture, gauze hangings for draperies of silks and brocade. The inner hall of almost every house, it is true, is furnished in European style — exiles love to surround themselves with remembrances of their far-away home. But, though very pretty, this room is generally empty of inhabitants, except, perhaps, for an hour now and then, during the rainy season. For, in this climate, to sit in a velvet chair is to realize the sensations of Saint Laurence, without the sustaining consciousness of martyrdom. — For the sake of coolness again, one gets up at half-past five, or six, at the very latest, keeps indoors till sunset, sleeps away the hot hours of the afternoon on a bed which it requires experience and a delicate sense of touch to distinguish from a deal board, and spends the better part of one's waking existence in the bath room.

*Ice vendors in Batavia*

# The White Rajahs of Borneo

The Brooke Dynasty reigned on the island of Borneo from 1841 to 1946. James Brooke, an Englishman, was the first monarch and founded the Kingdom of Sarawak in northern Borneo when it was given to him by the Sultanate of Brunei for work done against pirates and rebellion. Brooke received independent kingdom status for Sarawak and was ruled by his family, called the White Rajahs, until the territory was ceded to the United Kingdom in 1946. Most of the rest of the island was part of the Dutch East Indies except for a very small territory in the very north under the control of the British government.

*The island of Borneo was split between the British in the North and the Dutch in the south following a treaty in 1824 meant to assert the spheres of influence of the two regional rivals.*

*Sir James Brooke, the first of the White Rajahs of the Kingdom of Sarawak in northern Borneo*

*The emblem of the Kingdom of Sarawak, ruled by the White Rajahs*

119

# My Lord, The Crocodile

Crocodiles have long infested the shores of Java and there have been many reports down the years of people being eaten by the animals . In an attempt to solve the problem, the Dutch government once offered a reward for every carcass brought to the authorities though this plan ultimately failed. The following excerpt From Java Facts and Fancies by Augusta De Wit in 1905 relates a local tale of the crocodile.

The Malays, as a rule, do not readily kill crocodiles. They believe that the spirits of the dead are re-incarnated in these animals; so that, what seems a repulsive and dangerous beast, may, in reality, be an honoured father, or a long lamented bride. And they piously prefer the risk of being devoured to the certainty of becoming murderers. Far from injuring, they honour the "cayman" by sacrifices of rice, meat, and fruit, which they send down the river in little baskets of palm-leaves with a light twinkling a-top; a gift offered whenever a child is born, to propitiate the metamorphosed ancestors in river and sea, and implore their protection for this, their newly born descendant. Human feelings and susceptibilities are attributed to them which the Malay carefully abstains from wounding. He never speaks but of "My Lord the Crocodile." And a wayang-play, such as, for instance, Krokosono, the hero of which defeats and kills the King of the Crocodiles, no dalang would dream of representing in a place where caymans could hear or see it. There is one act, however, by which a crocodile forfeits all claim to respect: and that is killing a human being. From his supposed human nature, it evidently follows that this is an act of malice prepense, a crime knowingly committed; and, as such, should be punished as it would be were the perpetrator a man or a woman—that is, with death. It would seem too as if the guilty creature were conscious of his crime, and, sometimes, out of sheer remorse, gave himself up to justice. At least, a story to this effect is told of a certain crocodile, which had devoured a little girl, and this, though the child's parents had duly offered rice and meat and fruit, at the stated times; of which gifts this crocodile had undoubtedly had his share. The parents, weeping, sought a hermit who lived not far from the "dessa" or village, a wise man who understood the language of animals; and implored him to restore at least the remains of their daughter's little body to them, and to visit with condign punishment her brutal murderer. The hermit, moved with pity and indignation, forthwith left his cave, and repaired to the sea-shore. There, standing with his feet in the waves, he pronounced the potent spell which all crocodiles must obey. They came, hurrying, from far and near: the shore bristled with their scaly backs ranged in serried rank and file. When all were present, the hermit addressed them in their own tongue, declaring that one of them had committed the unpardonable crime of murder, murder upon an innocent child, whose parents had offered sacrifices for her at her birth: rice and fruit and meat, of which they all had partaken, in token of amity and good will. So abominable a breach of good faith should not be suffered to remain unpunished. Wherefore, let him who had perpetrated it, stand forth! But all the others, let them withdraw into the sea! The crocodiles heard. The solid land seemed to heave and break up, as the congregated thousands dispersed. But one crocodile remained behind on the beach. It crawled nearer and lay down at the feet of the hermit. And the father of the little girl, approaching, drew his "kris," and thrust it into the creature's eyes, killing it. The holy man then took out of the monster's jaws the necklace of blue beads, which the little girl had worn, and handed it to the father, promising him that, within the year, his wife would bear him another daughter, even fairer than the lost one.

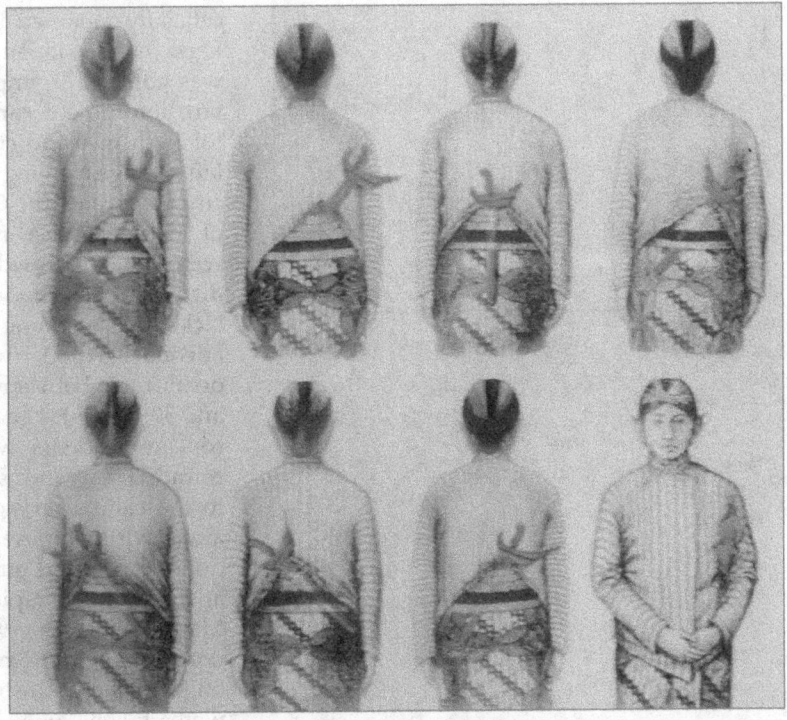

*Many ways to wear a kris in Javanese culture*

*The "kris" is a wavy-bladed dagger most commonly associated with the culture of Java, though it can be found throughout the surrounding islands. The dagger is used as a weapon as well as a spiritual object in ceremonies, an heirloom, a symbol of status or heroism, and some are even thought to possess special abilities or magical powers.*

# "The City of Hell"

Before WWII, the Dutch East Indies were in the midst of the Indonesian National Awakening, the beginning of the development of a national Indonesian identity outside of their Dutch colonists. So, when the Japanese began spreading the idea that they were the "Light of Asia," the Indonesians were initially hopeful that the Japanese invasion would remove the Dutch system. Instead the Japanese replaced the old system with one that, at its end, was even more brutal. From 1942 to 1945, Batavia, officially renamed Djakarta by the Japanese, was home to 16 important internment camps for both war and civilian hostages, giving the city the name "the City of Hell". These camps were overcrowded, dirty, diseased, and lacked clean water or adequate food with death rates between 13 and 30 percent. The European residents were rounded up and sent to the camps on sight, along with Chinese Indonesians found guilty against the occupiers. Many residents were not just sent to the prison camps but instead were taken away as forced laborers – called romusha – or to work as sex slaves. Many were submitted to tor-

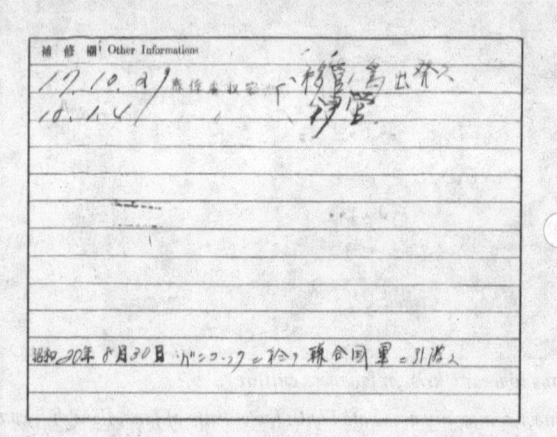

*Registration Card from the Japanese Occupation*

ture that included burning with cigarettes, placing a pencil or stick between the fingers and squeezing or, more severe, electric shocks or forcing the accused to drink a pail or water and the interrogator standing on his stomach. A later United Nations report has estimated that around 4 million people in Indonesia died as a result of starvation and forced labor over the Japanese occupation.

The Japanese also dismantled much of the infrastructure within the cities. Railway lines, metal statues, and any other useful materials were pulled out and used for the Japanese war effort. While the destruction of many of the Dutch colonial statues was welcomed by the Indonesians, the cities were left in economic decline and disrepair.

Towards the end of the Japanese rule, the occupying government began to support Indonesian nationalistic movements in an attempt to gain support and mobilize the people against the Allied forces. Where before the Japanese had banned nationalistic discussions and the use of the Indonesian flag, they were now supporting nationalist leaders such as Sukarno and Hatta and providing Indonesian youth with military training and weapons for a volunteer army. This training, along with the destruction of most of the Dutch colonial state, became an invaluable resource following the war for the National Revolution. The occupation ended in 1945 following the Japanese surrender, the Allied powers were unwilling to risk an invasion during the war, and Indonesia was once again a Dutch colonial state. This rule, however, was not to last as the Indonesians declared independence and the Indonesian National Revolution began.

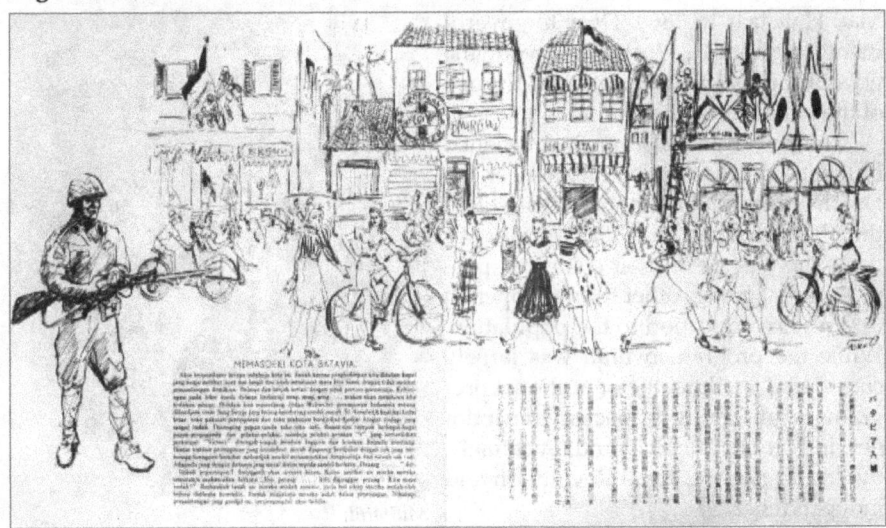

# Multatuli

Born Eduard Douwes Dekker in 1820, the Dutch writer known as Multatuli is perhaps most famous for his satirical criticism of the Dutch colonial system in the East Indies in a book called *Max Havelaar*. In this somewhat-autobiographical novel, Multatuli tells the story of an idealistic Dutch colonial officer determined to make changes to help the local people he is in charge of. Eventually the officer's plans go from bad to worse as abuses of the locals only continue and he realizes just how out of touch he is.

Multatuli began his career as a civil servant in the Dutch East Indies on the island of Java, later in the Moluccas, and finally in Bantam. Due to his open speech against the colonial system and its abuses, he was threatened with dismissal, resigned, and moved back to the Netherlands where he eventually published Max Havelaar in 1860. Despite government attempts to block its spread, the novel brought awareness across Europe of the injustices in the Dutch colonies.

The novel was also an instrumental influence on the implementation of the Dutch Ethical Policy in 1901 that stated that the Dutch had an ethical responsibility to the welfare of their colonized peoples and, among other things, opened up Western education to the population. While the program overall was largely considered a failure, the educational programs significantly impacted the Indonesian National Revival and, eventually, the Indonesian National Revolution and independence.

*Multatuli*

# Bataviaasch Nieuwsblad

Paulus Adrianus Daum, commonly known as P.A. Daum was a Dutch author who spent much of his life in the East Indies. He started his career in Semarang, a city on the northern coast of Java, as the editor-in-chief of Indisch Vaderland in 1883. Following disagreements with the authorities over anti-colonialism statements, Daum fled to Batavia where he founded another newspaper, the Bataviaasch Nieuwsblad (Batavia News). Under Daum's leadership, it grew to be one of the largest newspapers in the Dutch East Indies with a reputation for giving a voice to native residents of the colony.

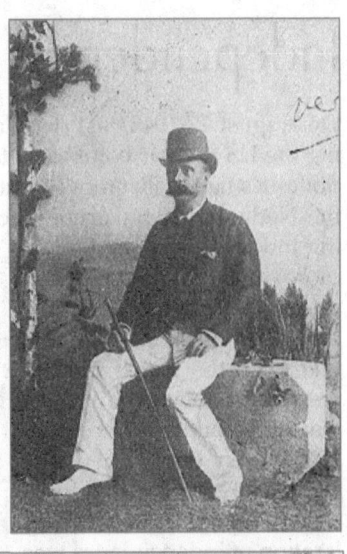

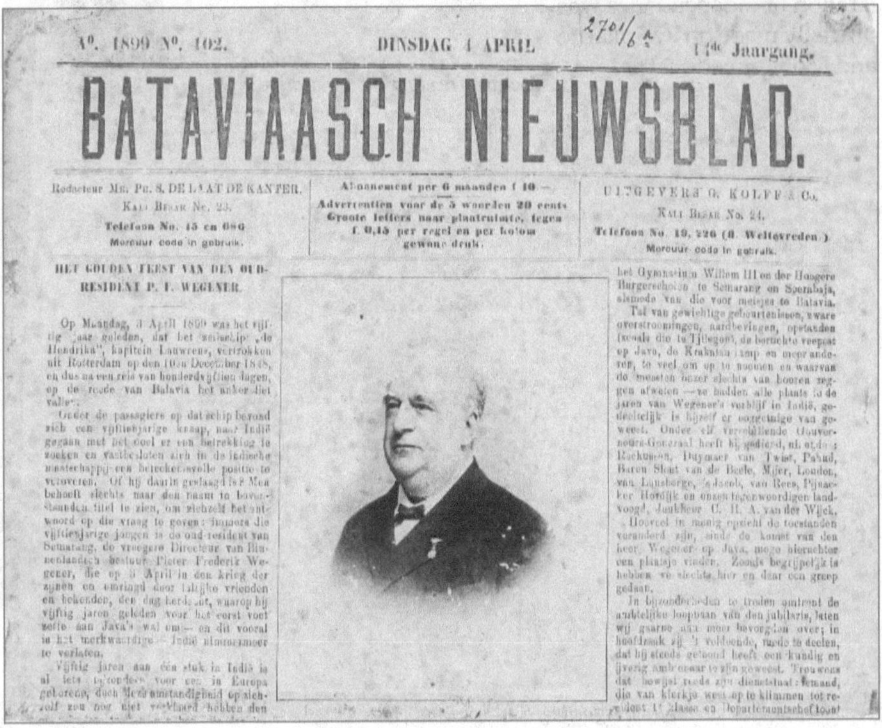

A°. 1899 N°. 102. DINSDAG 4 APRIL 2701/6 14[de] Jaargang.

BATAVIAASCH NIEUWSBLAD.

Redacteur Mr. Pr. S. DE LAAT DE KANTER.
Kali Besar No. 23.
Telefoon No. 15 en 686
Morcuur code in gebruik.

Abonnement per 6 maanden f 10.—
Advertentien voor de 5 woorden 20 cents
Groote letters naar plaatruimte, tegen
f. 0,15 per regel en per kolom
gewone druk.

UITGEVERS G. KOLFF & Co.
Kali Besar No. 24.
Telefoon No. 19, 226 (B. Weltevreden.)
Morcuur code in gebruik.

HET GOUDEN FEEST VAN DEN OUD-RESIDENT P. F. WEGENER.

Op Maandag, 3 April 1899 was het vijftig jaar geleden, dat het zeilschip „de Hendrika", kapitein Lauwrens, vertrokken uit Rotterdam op den 10en December 1848, en dus na een reis van honderdvijftien dagen, op de reede van Batavia het anker liet vallen.

Onder de passagiers op dat schip bevond zich een vijftienjarige knaap, naar Indië gegaan met het doel er een betrekking te zoeken en vastbesloten zich in de Indische maatschappij een beteekenisvolle positie te veroveren. Of hij daarin geslaagd is? Men behoeft slechts naar den naam te bovenstaanden titel te zien, om zichzelf het antwoord op die vraag te geven: immers die vijftienjarige jongen is de oud-resident van Semarang, de vroegere Directeur van Binnenlandsch bestuur Pieter Frederik Wegener, die op 3 April in den krieg der zijnen en omringd door talrijke vrienden en bekenden, den dag herdacht, waarop hij vijftig jaren geleden voor het eerst voet zette aan Java's wal om — en dit vooral is het merkwaardige — Indië nimmermeer te verlaten.

Vijftig jaren aan één stuk in Indië is al iets bijzonders voor een in Europa geborene, doch deze omstandigheid op zichzelf zou nog niet verklaard hebben den

het Gymnasium Willem III en der Hoogere Burgerscholen te Semarang en Soerabaja, alsmede van die voor meisjes te Batavia.

Tal van gewichtige gebeurtenissen, zware overstroomingen, aardbevingen, opstanden (zooals die te Tjilegon), de beruchte veepest op Java, de Krakatau-ramp en meer andere, te veel om op te noemen en waarvan de meesten onzer slechts van hooren zeggen afweten — ze hadden alle plaats in de jaren van Wegener's verblijf in Indië, gedeeltelijk is hijzelf er ooggetuige van geweest. Onder elf verschillende Gouverneurs-Generaal heeft hij gediend, nl. onder: Rochussen, Duymaer van Twist, Pahud, Baron Sloet van de Beele, Mijer, Loudon, van Lansberge, 's Jacob, van Rees, Pijnacker Hordijk en onzen tegenwoordigen landvoogd, Jonkheer C. H. A. van der Wijck.

Hoeveel in menig opzicht de toestanden veranderd zijn, sinds de komst van den heer Wegener op Java, moge hierachter een plaatsje vinden. Zooals begrijpelijk is hebben we slechts hier en daar een greep gedaan.

In bijzonderheden te treden omtrent de ambtelijke loopbaan van den jubilaris, laten wij gaarne aan meer bevoegden over; in hoofdzaak zij 't voldoende, mede te deelen, dat hij steeds getoond heeft een kundig en ijverig ambtenaar te zijn geweest. Trouwens dat bewijst reeds zijn dienststaat: iemand, die van klerkje wist op te klimmen tot resident 1e klasse en Departementschef toont

# Independence

On August 17 1945, just two days after Japan's unconditional surrender following the US nuclear bombing attacks on the cities of Hiroshima and Nagasaki, Indonesia's nationalist movement headed by Sukarno declared independence from the Netherlands. Sukarno, who became, the first president of Indonesia following independence, had spent more than a decade in prison under the Dutch prior to the Japanese invasion. With the war over, the Dutch tried to re-establish their rule, and the war only ended in December 1949 when the Netherlands formally recognized Indonesia's independence. The declaration of independence was officially made on by Sukarno and Mohammad Hatta.

*Soekarno reading the declaration*

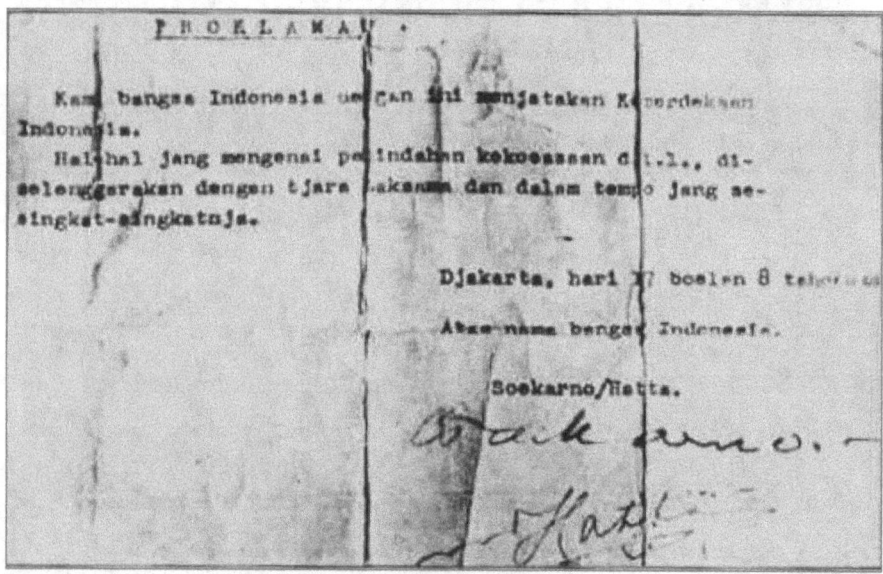

*The independence declaration signed by Soekarno and Hatta*

# PROCLAMATION

WE THE PEOPLE OF INDONESIA HEREBY
DECLARE THE INDEPENDENCE OF INDONESIA.
MATTERS WHICH CONCERN THE TRANSFER OF
POWER AND OTHER THINGS WILL BE EXECUTED
BY CAREFUL MEANS AND IN THE SHORTEST
POSSIBLE TIME.

DJAKARTA, 17 AUGUST 1945
IN THE NAME OF THE PEOPLE OF INDONESIA
SOEKARNO – HATTA